How to Make Money from
Travel Writing

Visit our How To website at www.howto.co.uk

At **www.howto.co.uk** you can engage in conversation with our authors – all of whom have 'been there and done that' in their specialist fields. You can get access to special offers and additional content but most importantly you will be able to engage with, and become a part of, a wide and growing community of people just like yourself.

At **www.howto.co.uk** you'll be able to talk and share tips with people who have similar interests and are facing similar challenges in their lives. People who, just like you, have the desire to change their lives for the better – be it through moving to a new country, starting a new business, growing their own vegetables, or writing a novel.

At **www.howto.co.uk** you'll find the support and encouragement you need to help make your aspirations a reality.

You can go direct to **ww.how-to-make-money-from-travel-writing.co.uk** which is part of the main How To site.

How To Books strives to present authentic, inspiring, practical information in their books. Now, when you buy a title from **How To Books,** you get even more than just words on a page.

How to Make Money from
Travel Writing

**Practical advice on turning the dream
into a well-paid reality**

SARAH WOODS

Published by How To Books Ltd,
Spring Hill House, Spring Hill Road,
Begbroke, Oxford OX5 1RX. United Kingdom.
Tel: (01865) 375794. Fax: (01865) 379162.
info@howtobooks.co.uk
www.howtobooks.co.uk

How To Books greatly reduce the carbon footprint of their books by sourcing their
typesetting and printing in the UK.

British Library Cataloguing in Publication Data
A catalogue record for this book is available from the British Library

ISBN 978 1 84528 394 0

Produced for How To Books by Deer Park Productions, Tavistock, Devon
Typeset by PDQ Typesetting, Newcastle-under-Lyme, Staffs.
Printed and bound by Cromwell Press Group, Trowbridge, Wiltshire

NOTE: The material contained in this book is set out in good faith for general guidance
and no liability can be accepted for loss or expense incurred as a result of relying in
particular circumstances on statements made in the book. The laws and regulations are
complex and liable to change, and readers should check the current position with the
relevant authorities before making personal arrangements.

Contents

Introduction

When I was a young girl, I would curl up in bed with an old transistor radio and twiddle the dial until it found the BBC's World Service. On the pretence of slumber, I would listen to the crackling sounds of exotic-sounding foreign lands and marvel at the reportage from countries I never knew existed. With my encyclopaedia by my side, I'd look up far-flung isles and continents. It wasn't long before I'd pinpointed an elaborate string of nations that I felt warranted personal exploration. I drew up maps and read books detailing the earliest accounts of travel, from the vivid tales of Marco Polo's forays along the Silk Road, to the harrowing escapades and exploits of Christopher Columbus and Walter Raleigh. Losing myself in Charles Darwin's diaries, I dreamt of ancient indigenous tribes and unworldly beasts in forebidding jungles. Mark Twain roused an early fascination with following the equator and Henry Morgan a lifelong curiosity in journeying the high seas. By the age of ten, I had started writing fictional narratives of my own make-believe journeys across lands imagined – but still unseen.

When I read Paul Theroux's first travel book, *The Great Railway Bazaar*, in my early 20s, I consumed each page with passion, realising my ravenous appetite for the author's cynical observations as he further fuelled my imagination for the places brought to me by my shortwave radio a decade or more before. By now, my attempts at writing had given way to priorities of adulthood – yet Theroux's narratives spurred me on to book a ticket to Australia on a whim – and I never looked back. Next Asia, the US and the Caribbean before criss-crossing Europe as one destination after another turned the armchair travel dreams of an infant into my coming of age. I read every piece of travel

literature I could get my hands on, from Bruce Chatwin in
Patagonia and records of ancient pilgrimages, to family trips in
antiquity and the middle ages.

It took a while to dawn on me that I could follow in their
footsteps. But once I realised that I could see the world and sell
the story, it opened up the globe. I got some business cards
printed and declared myself a travel writer. Viewing the planet as
my workplace, I pledged that if I could get to a place, I would
write about it – simple as that. Employing a mix of zeal, pluck,
tenacity and luck, I forged contacts and won contracts and
commissions. Fortuitously, new airlines sprung up to journey to
hitherto unknown places as the world began to get more easily
navigable. My short hops turned to long jaunts and I was soon a
perpetual traveller who searched out places on the map. I
struggled with faxing copy and gathering research in public
libraries, but then a new-fangled invention arrived to help me –
the internet. Few modern technologies have aided travel writers
more.

Today, two decades on, I'm still journeying for up to 200 days per
year. I am also earning a decent income whilst doing something I
truly, truly adore. Making a living solely from travel writing isn't
easy – but it is possible. In the past 20 years, I've been paid to
spear-fish in the inky-green shallows of the Amazon River,
thrown pots with sculptors in Panama's Herrera Province, cruised
the Caribbean waters in luxury, and enjoy a nostalgic journey on
the oh-so-romantic Orient Express. I have visited over 50
countries (clocking up over three quarter of a million kilometres
en route) and I've dined with kings, queens and prime ministers
in sumptuous opulence, and eaten around an open fire with tribal
chiefs. I've met Balinese healers, Cypriot cheese-makers, Tibetan

chess masters, Spanish horse breeders, Chinese scribes, Sri Lankan tea growers and Japanese geisha.

I have witnessed firsthand the incredible cultural diversity of our planet and have been humbled by successive acts of human kindness. People have been generous and gracious, from the patrons of Santa Monica's glitzy sidewalk diners, to the street sweepers in the low-class barrios of Colombia. I've made lifelong friends from Norway to Nicaragua and I've learned a lot about the world in which we live – and also about myself. Hilaire Belloc once said: 'We wander for distraction, but we travel for fulfilment' – and, for me, it is thrilling to feel so wholly fulfilled.

Yet travel writing isn't just about the journeys and experiences – there's the hard work of putting pen to paper to contend with. This can mean hours, or days or weeks, sitting huddled over a keyboard willing a story to emerge from a brain that is jet-lagged. Balancing time differences can also be the source of deadline conundrums. I was once commissioned by a Panamanian editor working in Spain who mistakenly assumed I was in Singapore when I was actually in Australia. It took me half a morning to work out that I only had two hours to write a piece despite a four-day leeway. After a 38-hour journey home, when all you want to do is sleep, there's the stress of looming deadlines and a constant stream of emails to deal with. Good travel writers are disciplined and business-minded – it's not all about talent. Finding work, retaining clients and providing good customer service are important in an editor-contributor relationship.

Much like any job, it's not all glamour and glory – so being timely, efficient and reliable can be as important as delivering creative copy. If you write on the road, like me, you may also need to muster up descriptions of one place whilst travelling through another. I've written about Poland's snow-capped mountains whilst journeying through the sweltering South African bush. I've also become adept at knuckling down to 1,000 words in airport lounges, noisy internet cafes and borrowed desk space – when what you really need is solitude, peace and quiet. Today, my constant companions are the writings of a new breed of travel author, from Polly Evans in New Zealand and John Malathronas in South Africa, to Charlie Connelly's rhinestone-clad tales of roving in Memphis.

In this book, I attempt to provide aspiring travel writers with the tools to maximise their experiences – and their incomes. It's not always about the money, of course, as travel is a currency that brings its own rich rewards. However, those keen to make a living as a wandering scribe will find plenty of tips and advice to help them profit. There are also valuable contributions from many of the UK's finest travel-writing talent, from award-winning feature writers and authors, to editors and publishers. Travel PRs add their own valuable insight into the practical help they can provide, while experts in online content, newspapers, magazines and guidebooks explore the varied possibilities travel writing offers. As a travel writer you may well be offered first-class seats on your choice of airline or a $10,000-a-night suite without charge – but rarely do these happen without a credible reputation and reliable mode of work.

The aim of this book is to help nurture success in those dedicated to their professions – I only wish a similar guide had been available when I started out. I assumed that a love of travel and a love of writing was enough – and it can be, of course. However, this book leaves little to chance: offering practical know-how to demystify the travel writing market whilst tackling the thorny issue of payment head on.

Fewer geographical limits and open borders ensure it has never been a better time to roam the planet. Allow this book to guide you through jargon, jungles and genres as it journeys through a myriad possibilities outlined in chapters created to hone your skills. Of roving to faraway places, St Augustine once said that 'the World is a book – and those who do not travel read only a page'. This book is designed to help anyone with a yen for travel and adventure, and a desire to capture the essence of travel in words, stories and pages. So reminisce, reflect and explore new themes – you'll be surprised where it can lead.

Thank You

Some of the hardest working travel writers, publishers, editors and authors have been generous with their time in the writing of this book. Very special thanks go to Adrian Phillips, Kathi Hall, Ross Hilton, Ray Carmen, Roger Norum, John Malathronas, Heloise Crowther, Polly Evans, Cathy Smith, Melissa Shales, Anna Moores, Kathryn Peel, Jennifer Barclay, Ginny Cummings, Susie Tempest, Jon Cunningham, Richard Human, Sadie Smith, Emma Field, Alison Booth, Vanessa Aves, Gillian Thornton, Juan Carlos Eleno, Jonathan Loirie, Mark Henshall, Dan Linstead, Vicky Baker, Ashley Jack, Bryn Williams, Sonia Soltani, Anna Maria Espsäter, Francis Booth, Bryn Frank, Raichel Phipps, Ashley Gibbins, Alessandra Smith, Fiona Quinn, Mike Unwin, April Hutchinson, Hilary Bradt, Juan Guillermo Perez, Gary Buchanan, Helen Truszkoswki, Liz Jarvis, Robin Mead, Rosemary Bailey, Victoria Trott, Lisa Gerard-Sharp and Linda Jackson. With deep gratitude also to Jacqui McCarthy, the British Guild of Travel Writers and everyone involved in the Small World Foundation. Of course, I'm forever indebted to my friends and family who put up with my continued, prolonged absences with good humour and considerable patience.

With thanks also to Mr Armitage without whom none of this would be possible.

Dedication

For Mr Armitage, an erudite and expressive educator at Stratton Upper School, Biggleswade – and a man who took the time to dig deep and encourage my early writing. He also brought vivid colour to an altogether dreary, unimaginative establishment, livening up a shabby beige decor with a succession of lurid pink shirts, bright red ties, shiny slip-on mules and wicker shopping baskets, not to mention cutting wit.

Also for Matthew and Joseph.

Travel Writing: Fact or Fiction?

WHAT IS TRAVEL WRITING?

> ❝ *To my mind, the greatest reward and luxury of travel is to be able to experience everyday things as if for the first time, to be in a position in which almost nothing is so familiar it is taken for granted.* ❞

Bill Bryson

I've lost count of the number of times I've heard 'I'd love to be a travel writer' from friends and acquaintances who don't actually know exactly what travel writing is. In truth, every good scribe brings something different to travel writing – yet for it to be commercially rewarding or income generating, a piece of travel writing needs to strike a chord with a broad scope of readers to illuminate or inspire, in one way or another.

That this isn't a guide that details *exactly* how to be a travel writer is a conscious move on my part. In my experience, people come to travel writing through many different paths for a wide variety of reasons. I've yet to read a guide to travel writing that has covered all of these reasons comprehensively. This is not a criticism of the publications themselves, but an observation of the broad base from which travel writers emerge. Some are journalists tired of penning hard news. Others are creative writers who move into travel. Many are travellers fuelled with enthusiasm to write about the incredible places and people they've met.

Depending on whom you ask, a travel writer is either:

◆ a creative talent;
◆ a lucky so-and-so with a dream job;
◆ a freeloading git.

Background to travel writers

Travel writers come from all walks of life. There is no single road of entry into the field of travel writing and it's more than possible to wander into it with very little training at all. However, most people want to write well, so they seek out the expertise of others and develop a global understanding. They study, labour and develop their craft to be the best. Some are hobbyists, happy that they are sharing their experiences through the written word. Others want to make a living from their writing and do everything they can to make this happen. *How to Make Money from Travel Writing* offers practical guidance on how to do this, from pitching ideas and creating productive and rewarding contacts, to implementing marketing strategies to build sales and develop a brand. It explores the importance of networking and maximising client relationships and offers step-by-step advice on how to nurture ongoing income streams – paramount for modern travel writers keen to earn a decent crust.

Using your imagination

Travel writing involves imagination, legwork and a quizzical eye for detail to bring the experiences of a place or journey alive in a collection of words on a page. It requires the writer to put themselves in the shoes of the reader in order to deliver the mood, colour and information they need to transport them on an evocative jaunt.

Understanding the audience for your writing is crucial in determining exactly what level of detail is required in a genre that spans an extremely broad field. Good travel writing attempts to reverse the old cliché and to delve into what's new or lesser-known. Even the most travelled destinations at the hub of mass tourism offer millions of fresh, exciting little details, be it the aromas, hues, noises or character of their people. Good travel writing will seek these out to provide a new, evocative personal encounter and vibrant perspective. By shying away from the well-worn phrases and using first-hand observations, a writer can truly make their take on a place unique. Readers are hungry for titbits and this psychological need should drive a travel writer to 'go the extra mile' – both in their literary style and approach to journeying. By recording first impressions, detailing emotions and personal accounts, a writer will have a diverse range of material for use in many creative modes.

As a non-fiction category, travel writing relies heavily on a base of facts. However, as a genre, it can encompass nitty-gritty travelogues, journals and diaries, internet blogs and magazine features as well as newsy reports. It can span consumer publications and trade titles that demand very different writing skills and disciplines. Some articles require travel writing free from elaborate descriptions and narratives, requiring only fact-based reporting without prose or inflated vision. Others demand richly-told tales that interweave imagination with a certain amount of hyperbole. Most require a keen use of the senses fused with interactions, intuition and accuracy to convey the minutiae of detail that allows an experience to unfold. Memories are important, of course, but there is no substitute for scribbled down episodes, anecdotes and straight, hard facts. Even in a high-tech world, a writing pad remains the tried and tested concrete foundation on which most accounts are based. Of course, no single person can possibly absorb every detail but a travel writer should be prepared to try – speaking to as many people as possible and devouring a place with every sense to establish its mood, unique selling points (USPs, see page 122), spirit and appeal.

TRAVEL AS TRAVEL WRITER

◆ Have a plan, but travel with a fluid flexibility that allows you to divert from the schedule and linger in places rich in material. Don't dither unnecessarily though – use your time wisely to gather information but keep your eyes open for stories that may crop up en route.

◆ Speak to as many locals as possible about their home town and region, from its history to its people. Ask for local proverbs, myths and legends and get them to describe the characteristics of the locals. Choose a wide cross-section of people, from a waiter, cabbie and desk clerk to someone at the local school, library or university. Don't talk too much, listen – and allow individual encounters to unfold.

◆ Ask for recommendations on places to eat like a local – not the usual tourist eateries or mainstream haunts, but the side-street diners favoured by the townsfolk.

◆ Fully familiarise yourself with your location – study maps and read the local newspapers so that you know exactly where you are and what's going on around you. Watching the morning news will help you strike up casual conversions with local people, while knowing how a location sits in geographic terms will enable you to site yourself in relation to airports, main roads, rivers and the sea – all important in travelling terms.

◆ Try to travel as the local people do – walk, or take the bus or hire a bicycle in preference to a car; you'll see more and have a greater opportunity to maximise encounters as you go.

◆ Don't be tempted to pack too much into a single day – it will close your mind to sights, experiences and attractions that aren't on your schedule. Overdoing it will also exhaust you – and rushing around whilst clock-watching will impact on how you experience a place.

❝ MAKING THE GRADE

An Expert's View...

The travel and publishing industry is evolving rapidly, which presents opportunity. But it's a tough market, so writers need to be adaptable, committed and get the basics right.

Whether working in print or on digital content, editorial rigour is vital as you are showcasing your expertise. Be punctual, take on feedback, focus on the detail of a commission and establish an efficient working relationship.

Always question and ask why*: how can this copy be improved and what do I mean to say here?*

Travel cliché formulas, laziness, lateness, lack of research, not following the specifics of a brief and a tangled maze of verbiage will not get you more work. Get it right though and the reader, editor and writer are happy.

Mark Henshall is a Brighton/London-based travel writer and editor and the first UK Commissioning Editor for Frommer's. Previously he was Deputy Editor of *ABTA Magazine* and has worked for Pearson, the European Commission in France and consumer travel titles.

Today's travel writers can fully exploit a growing range of publishing outlets and opportunities, from newspaper travel sections, in-flight magazines, online content, books and travel literature, guidebooks and commercial campaigns (such as advertising material, marketing aids and tourist board initiatives). As a genre, it encapsulates Rough Guide reviews to some of the world's most powerful narrative non-fiction, as modern explorers tackle journeys across the familiar and the unknown.

In step with this expanding range of publishing opportunities are the ever-growing number of travel writing subjects, from practical service stories that provide readers with a round-up of a specific destination or travel-related topic (e.g. how-to articles, Top 10 beaches, resort reviews and the latest airline news), to destination pieces that portray the essence of a place in order to bring it to life to the reader.

Personal essays and narratives tend to centre on a specific, highly individual encounter – with a person, place or cultural aspect. By using the larger experiences of the writer, these specialised personal reflections can border on a travel memoir with humour intermingled with keen, precise observations with the character of the episode – and the writer – very much at the core. Yet regardless of the style of writing, the same principles of penning a good travel story apply.

At the heart of every newspaper or magazine feature, travel book or guide is a single fundamental – the place. Whatever you write, however you write, it is this that should be richly conveyed to the reader. Absorbing writing uses the crafting structure of a short story to allow the reader to step in the writer's shadow and be carried up, up – and away.

> ## ❛ FROM THE SOFA TO EVEREST BASE CAMP
>
> **An Expert's View**...
>
> *The best travel writing engages all five senses to fire the reader's imagination and allow them to take the trip in their mind. It is the rare person who has the time and/or money to partake of all the travel opportunities presented in one magazine (or even one newspaper section), so your feature might be the only route the reader has from their sofa to Everest Base Camp or Harry's Bar in Venice. With that in mind, I prefer not to bump into the writer while I'm mentally following my Sherpa up the slopes or coolly sipping my Bellini. The piece should be focused on what the reader could be doing, not what the writer just did. There are exceptions to this rule, of course, but not as many as one might think. Practical details are best at the end or in a separate box – I want the reader to be fully intoxicated by the experience before they see the bar bill.* ❜
>
> American-born Kathi Hall is Managing Editor at the London offices of Story Worldwide. (Visit: www.storyworldwide.co.uk)

TRAVEL WRITING STYLES

It pays to scour the newspaper and magazine stands, bookshelves and internet to gain a better insight into the differences between the following. This legwork is an invaluable tool and will help new writers gather background research into styles, tones and structures. Making a cuttings book of particularly good examples of travel stories can also help in getting a feel for what works for you – and what doesn't. It will also clarify how certain subjects are tackled, the destinations that are hot topics and how different writers craft their pieces to reach out to readers with specific interests. Use it as a reference point for the subtle use of prose, a good flow of words and the supple creative dexterity in which detail is strung together with exacting detail or factual observations. For samples of the following, see Appendix 3.

Personal essays

This enduring style of writing has its origins in ancient literature and remains a popular form today. Told in the first person, it is highly individual as only you can write it – ensuring a wholly unique account of a place or encounter, even if it has been written about a million times. Drawing on experiences, impressions, observations and discoveries, the personal essay unfolds using insight and a deep human connection. Forming a bond with the reader, who is encouraged to identify with the writer, it uses comparisons, humour, irony and allusions to nurture a sense of recognition – even if the subject is new.

Personal essays appear to have been written with effortless ease, yet they require considerable thought and are often the most labour-intensive travel articles to compose. Balancing personal experiences in a context of circumstance using neutral facts peppered with opinion isn't easy to perfect. Generally speaking, it is often mastered by writers of maturity who can establish trust with the reader through complex crafting, an authoritative tone, precise detailing, well-timed irony and a self-aware elegance of prose.

Destination pieces

As one of the most popular styles of travel writing, destination pieces explore a place within the structure of a theme or angle but offer a broad overview nonetheless. Because of this, they often explore a well-travelled, reliable tourist route – such as Spain, France or Florida – but rather than a repetitive destination round-up, the story is wrapped up in a specific subject matter, e.g. Andalusia's San Juan Festival, Burgundy's Wine Harvest or Christmas Shopping in Orlando's Discount Malls. Yet unlike the special interest piece (see page 11) it doesn't focus solely on a specific activity, offering general tourist information aimed at broad appeal.

The opening (lead) paragraph is used to set the scene: why the writer is there and where the place is with some enticing facts to whet the reader's appetite. With all destination pieces, the opening is crucial – in just a few lines it needs to drive home the 'why?', 'who?' and 'where?'. It may outline the characters that are central to the piece and will almost always be written in narrative form with the writer's presence subdued (but may occasionally use or introduce the first person). Using a confiding tone, the reader is made to feel privy to the motivation and desires of the writer.

To this end, a destination piece should be colourful, evocative and tempting, with plenty to offer on much-written about destinations that begs them to be rediscovered. Much like an armchair tour, it should guide a reader through the reasons why it is a place worthy of visit. Like a personal essay, it attempts to identify with the reader by using engaging copy that alludes to the type of person the destination appeals to.

Humour can be used in this style of story-telling with insight into its popularity, spiced with useful facts on where to go, who to see and what not to miss.

A DREAM JOB, SOMETIMES

An Expert's View...

*'How glamorous' people say 'to be a travel writer.' True... seeing the world at the expense of others, champagne and cocktails, eight-course tasting menus with fine wines, personal butlers, facials and body massages, **is** being a tad pampered. And luxury cruises, five-star accommodation with a private pool, limousine travel, and personal guides, **do** make life that little more enjoyable. Wildlife safaris in Africa, sailing the Caribbean on luxury yachts, rounding up cattle in Arizona, and hot-air ballooning over French mountains are awesome leisure pursuits, but as for this 'glamorous' malarkey...*

*Airport check-in at 4.30am, return at 2am, on no-frills flights, visiting summer 'hotspots' out of season and deserted skiing resorts in summer, spending hours at lunch and getting to picturesque destinations when the light has gone, are **not** amusing. Changed itineraries on arrival, no-show by local representatives, over-ambitious dawn to dusk excursion schedules and, as a 'treat', visiting private buildings not open to the general public, are* *exasperating. Dining alone draws unwanted attention, fellow travellers can't be chosen, sharing a room with a previously unknown journalist is a possibility, and sexist attitudes by men on golf press trips are not pleasant . . . eating pigs' ears and other specialities are often difficult to stomach, and just don't think about 'health and safety' on organised activities.* 〝

Linda Jackson started her freelance travel-writing career when she returned to the UK after years of living and working in Belgium, Dubai, Barbados, Morocco and France. Her travel writing covers a wide range of topics and destinations and has been published in numerous lifestyle magazines, the national press, and various golf, in-flight, and online publications. An accomplished photographer, Linda's images are also regularly published. She is based in south-east England, within easy reach of central London.
(Visit: www.linda-jackson.co.uk)

Special interest articles

This style of travel writing is aimed at travellers with a specific interest or hobby, be it serious scuba divers and vintage train enthusiasts or holidaymakers with a penchant for bric-a-brac markets. It focuses on specific activities as they relate to the travel experience and informs readers how they can pursue them while in the holiday mode. From cross-stitch sewing in Austria and spa-going in the Czech Republic, to antique collecting in Toronto and tangoing in Buenos Aires – the possibilities are endless. Mainstream publications may commission special interest articles to coincide with a major event or festival. However, with many thousands of special interest magazines published across the world, a key outlet for special interest travel articles is within titles that cater for each leisure pursuit.

Writers of special interest pieces are usually familiar with the subject or are clearly approaching the subject as a novice keen to try their hand. Golfing, horse-riding, caravanning, surfing and ballroom dancing are popular special interest topics – but no amount of research can be a substitute for first-hand knowledge. Get the terminology wrong or the context skewed and the credibility of the writer is immediately questioned – a turn-off for a reader expecting credibility. Special interest articles are often packed with facts, often in the form of a sidebar or panel. Generally speaking, the writer assumes a tone that accepts the reader is well-versed with the subject – unless the piece is being published in a mainstream publication.

Journey pieces

The essence of a journey piece is to describe the act of journeying with the emphasis on the mode of travel, be it donkey, train, canoe or rickshaw. Many awe-inspiring travel pieces centre on steam-powered paddle ships along the Mississippi River. Others meander along the vine-trimmed lanes of the South of France on bicycles with panniers stuffed with bottles of wine. Journeying is conveyed in all its glory, from the romance of leisurely gypsy caravans to the white-knuckle thrills of a tuk tuk across traffic-strewn streets. In many ways this style of writing conjures up the nostalgia of the grand old age of travel – even when it is tackling a 21st century subject, such as Japan's futuristic high speed monorails.

With mood and ambience at the forefront, a journey piece may only touch on the destination but will often draw on historical comparisons and involve liberal amounts of humour. Using a strong personal narrative, the story pulls the reader along for the ride through scenery, encounters and mishaps. It will almost certainly offer advice and tips from a first-hand perspective with references to strange queuing habits or timetable anomalies, for example.

Comments and observations provide an insight to fellow travellers while a sidebar panel generally tackles the specifics of trip planning.

❛ HOW TO GET COMMISSIONED?

An Expert's View...

Just follow these steps. First, immerse yourself in the publication you're targeting: note the types of features, usual word lengths and format, and what has already been covered. Is the style chatty, discursive or first person? Then send in a lively precis of around three topics – preferably catchy ideas reflecting trends or new developments (rather than just a destination). Stress your unique expertise in this area – why you, not someone else. Follow up with a reminder if necessary. Always write to length and be super-accurate. Remember that editors are always looking out for fresh, new writers. Et voila! ❜

Alison Booth has worked as an editor and writer on magazines with a strong travel element since 1977. She is currently editor of *Orient-Express Magazine* (International) for Orient-Express hotels, trains and cruises and *Orient-Express Magazine* (Asia) for the Eastern & Oriental Express train in South-East Asia. (Visit: www.orient-express.com)

Service articles

Readers across the world have a healthy appetite for travel advice and how-to articles, be it how to pack in less than half an hour or how to get the best flight deals online. Topics such as travel health, cultural etiquette and best-buy holiday gadgets form the basis of thousands of travel articles each year, from 'Top 10s' that highlight the airline reliability or in-flight meals, to exposés on holiday resort swimming pool cleanliness that provide readers with the inside scoop. At the core of these service articles is good, solid up-to-date research combined with expert comment from suitably qualified, credible industry spokespersons. Information is usually conveyed through intense, detail-orientated source material and is often balanced with a reference to a first-hand personal experience from the writer – such as a lesson learnt. Though the crux of a service piece may be a negative experience (lost luggage, a disastrous holiday or an airline that has gone bust) – the writer will highlight ways to avoid these woes. In the 'Top 10' articles, the opening paragraph sets the scene as to why the list has been compiled – reaching out to the reader on the basis that it is offering help.

News pegs

A wide variety of hot topics can form the foundation of a travel story, from aspects such as conflict, economic melt-downs, terrorist activity and a headline-grabbing archaeological discovery, to the Olympic Games, FIFA World Cup, celebrity Himalayan Trek for charity or Obama's lifting of sanctions in relation to Cuba.

A time-crucial alternative to the usual 'sun, sand and sea' travel piece, a news peg is based (sometimes quite loosely) on an event or breaking news item that makes a place worthy of greater media attention. In 2007, when 'missing' British canoeist John Darwin strolled into a police station in Cleveland claiming to have lost his memory, a connection with the Republic of Panama emerged as central to the plot. Never before has this tiny S-shaped squiggle of land in Central America received such global exposure as coverage

– initially a tabloid fraud story – spawned a series of Panama travel features across the world. Using John Darwin as a news peg on which to hang an article on the isthmus, Panama was explored in all its glory, from its 1,000 islands, golf and jungles, to its colonial architecture, diving and sandy beaches.

Other hot news topics that have generated similar coverage include the lost English backpacker in Australia's Blue Mountain region in 2009 and Alaska's rise to prominence in the travel pages thanks to the 2008 vice-presidential aspirations of Alaskan State Governor Sarah Palin.

The round-up

A round-up article is basically a fleshed-out list of short, snappy information that hones in on the pertinent points in a series of punchy teasers. Style-wise, it suits online content as well as magazine and newspaper travel sections. Writing needs to be tight as round-ups generally rely on a concise paragraph (or two) on each topic. Catchy sub-headings draw the reader while just enough useful and interesting information provides an incentive to research the idea further. In essence, a round-up is simply a collection of short snippets about places linked by a common thread before a mini-profile of the core elements and contacts (telephone, fax, email or web address) to allow the reader to find out more.

Round-up travel articles offer a seemingly infinite array of possibilities with destinations, interests and experiences used in umpteen different ways. By combining your own specific areas of knowledge, variations on a theme are almost endless. Brainstorm using a list of superlatives and other descriptors, e.g. best, hottest, most, friendliest, cleanest, newest, easiest, quickest, etc., or play around with numbers (5 best or top 10) and other group definitions (families, honeymooners, baby boomers) or catchy tags (Going Green: Mexico's Top Eco Havens). For example:

- London's Best Cheap-Eat Vegetarian Food Joints;
- Florida's Best Beaches for Families;
- Strange But True: Europe's Weirdest Museums;
- Asia's Finest Luxury Spas;
- Seven Environmental Wonders of the World;
- Pecs in the City: The Gyms of New York;
- Love Islands: Exclusive Island Vacations for Honeymooners;
- Rooms With a View: World's Finest High-Rise Hotels;
- Grape Escapes: France's Vineyard Retreats;
- Excess Baggage: Ten Essential Travel Packing Tips.

Travel blogs

More than 133 million blogs lurk in cyberspace now – many of them travel related. The growth of these online travel journals owes much to one of the web's first online diaries 'A Hypertext Journal' (1996) by artists Nina Pope and Karen Guthrie, who followed the route of Boswell and Johnson's 'Tour of the Western Isles' whilst responding to ongoing requests and interactions with their remote online audience.

Although many travel blog formats offer little opportunity for income-generating editorial submissions, some do much more than allow travellers to upload photos, map and archive their trips and meet like-minded souls. An ever-growing number of travel blog websites now publish articles and guides focusing on travel-related issues. This professional content often forms the basis of traveller discussions, debate and comment in the form of independent postings. Even large corporate entities are realising the power of the blog format with major banks, travel insurance companies and transport providers increasingly using this interactive media as a key component of their marketing drive. Online shared travel resources are continually rising to the challenge of the cut-and-thrust of the digital revolution.

Thousands of travel reviews and commentaries provide instant access to a wide array of first-hand travel experiences, from candid reviews and up-to-the-moment new developments to on-the-spot reports and breaking news.

❝ ONLINE AND OUT THERE

An Expert's View...

The internet is a great leveller. Chances are you're not going to get your writings published in Wanderlust *or* National Geographic *straight away. Instead, take some courses in web design and search engine optimisation and set up your own website. Once you've built up a bit of a following you have a valid outlet for publishing your own work. With publication guaranteed, you'll get a great response from online PR resources such as TravMedia and Response Source, meaning you can enhance your own travels by reviewing hotels, tours, etc. on the road. Plus, it will give you oodles of relevant experience in a highly competitive industry, making future commissions far more likely.* ❞

Emma Field learnt about travel writing from the inside out. A fast-track NCTJ qualification led to a job as editorial assistant with World Travel Guide. After working her way up to Acting Head of Editorial, Emma left to set up her own website (www.overlandtraveller.com) as she travels the world (again).

For bloggers themselves, online diaries are a great way to tell friends and family how a holiday is progressing more rapidly and in more detail than a 'wish you were here' postcard. Hundreds of travel blogs are launched each and every day – the following are some of the best at the time of writing:

aluxurytravelblog.com
Escape into the luxurious world of upscale travel in this blog dedicated to decadent journeying, from where to rub shoulders with the rich and famous and private jets to where to order the most expensive cocktail on the planet.

bravenewtraveler.com
This is a comprehensive site with numerous engaging threads about every aspect of worldwide journeying, from community initiatives and volunteering to the latest boutique hotel, plus travel-writer postings from individuals and grass-roots organisations.

crankyflier.com
Join a cultish following of this hugely popular consumer blog created by a self-confessed 'airline dork' to discover the inside scoop on Miami International's queuing system and plenty of survival tips for Heathrow's Terminal 5.

cruisecritic.co.uk
This fast-growing forum for cruise lovers contains information on cruise ships, destinations and tour options in more than 130 ports of call. It is also full of top-notch tips for specific cruising niches, from gay-only itineraries and partying to low-carbon cruises.

familytravellogue.com
Aimed squarely at family travellers, this popular forum is packed

with tips on how where to journey as an adventurous family group together with advice on foreign foods and nominations for the best children's travel books.

gadling.com
Prepare to be overwhelmed by this dazzling array of blogs that spans almost every country, activity and travel theme in the world. Comprehensive postings cover Albania to Australia with indepth reviews that provide advice on everything from bungee jumping to buying fine antiques, together with a host of entertaining holidaymaker podcasts and vodcasts.

gridskipper.com
Delve into comprehensive coverage of city hot spots updated with staggering frequency by a team of in-the-know contributors with their fingers on the pulse. Beautifully designed and easily navigable, Gridskipper scours the globe for hip hotels, vibey restaurants, happening nightlife and cool people with gorgeous photography and clear maps that take some beating.

intelligenttravel.typepad.com
This excellent sustainable travel blog is run by National Geographic's Intelligent Travel and offers a wealth of information on everything from the carbon-cutting skills of goats to the finest eco-tourism communities and traveller volunteer programmes.

jaunted.com
Comprehensive, well structured blog with pop travel culture as its focus – from the global naked security debate and hand luggage confusion to how to navigate Europe's train system with seamless ease.

thecoolhunter.co.uk/travel
Looking for the most creative, the most innovative, the newest, best and coolest in travel? Then check out this stylish hub for the best in swanky bars and restaurants with reviews of the world's chicest chichi hotels.

www.TheFoodExplorer.co.uk
Ever wanted to eat monkey brains, taste the best steak in the world, or find out which insects make the best eating? Then check out travel writer and author Catherine Quinn's excellent blog, which searches the globe for the greatest food experiences. Track the weird and unusual to the spectacular and sublime in this candid mission to bring you the world on a plate. Catherine also posts her own travel exploits at www.traverati.com where she showcases the best of travel writing, blogging and fact files on the web.

wayn.com
This large online community boasts more than 14 million members in 193 countries allowing members to meet and find people all around the world. Where Are You Now (WAYN) encourages travellers to share details of their upcoming trips such as information, guides, reviews and blogs – with an option to post accompanying photographs.

At the heart of good travel blog writing is lesser-known facts and information. So-called 'blogorrhea' – writing when you have nothing to say – is a real turn-off to readers. Nothing is duller than a trivial, dull encounter – so be sure to create an honest blog with a clearly defined purpose or angle. Be interesting, brave and honest, and give plenty of detail. Revealing unusual experiences will grab a reader's attention while using human emotions (fear, insecurities and stupidity) will help to create a bond between you, the writer, and the reader. The best posts are short, snappy and sassy so write tight and stick to the point.

To search for a travel blog on a particular subject, try: technorati.com/lifestyle.travel/, a search engine that tracks more than 30 million blogs, displaying entries that are most popular. Travolution.blogspot.com is similar. Google also has a search engine for blogs – click on the 'more' category in the search bar, then click 'blogs'.

> **Travel writing: 12 steps to get you started**
> Writers keen to work at maximum efficiency should consider the following as part of moving forward. There is no substitute for cultivating the senses, boosting writing confidence and being well informed and well prepared – but it is important to take the time to enjoy what you do. Also, allow for contingency time to ensure on-going flexibility to allow you to follow up story ideas on a whim.
>
> ◆ Write regularly, preferably at least three times a week in conjunction with keeping a journal.
>
> ◆ Expand your knowledge of writing styles and travel genres by reading a wide cross-section of different authors, both contemporary and classic, to explore the variety of fiction and non-fiction in travel writing.
>
> ◆ Become familiar with magazines and newspapers with travel sections. Save a number of travel websites in your internet 'favourites' file and stay abreast of what subjects and styles are being published.

◆ Check out maps, atlases, guidebooks and tourist-board websites for interesting attractions and landmarks. Stay abreast of tourism news, such as newly created National Parks and UNESCO status monuments and biospheres, and any changes in land frontiers or new airlines or transport routes.

◆ Be prepared, from the tools of your trade to a packing list and a bag of travel essentials. Make sure your travel jabs are up to date and gen-up on some handy foreign language basics. Have plenty of pens and a stock of journals at your disposal – and check that your passport is valid.

◆ Develop your senses. To expand your descriptive skills, write notes about the food you are eating, or about the noise of a traffic jam or a fairground you are experiencing. Spend time in a visually-stimulating location to test your ability to convey it in words. Smell as much as you can around you and try to describe it.

◆ Don't get bogged down in the routine of writing – a rigid structure on an ongoing basis can stifle creativity and be demotivating. Build in exciting pauses in the daily grind to allow for a stimulation of the senses. All manner of things can help to rejuvenate a travel writer, from a bus ride to a walk around a market, or a chat over coffee with a stranger.

◆ Consider having a medical check-up to gauge your general fitness, especially if you plan to engage in trekking at altitude, undertake a succession of long-haul flights or explore a jungle.

◆ Get your finances in order to ensure you are well placed to travel. Consider shopping around for credit cards with low rates of interest for expenses (preferable to carrying cash but sometimes suitable only for major cities) and for cash cards with zero fees or commission for withdrawing local currency all over the world.

- ◆ Create two email distribution lists – one of clients and potential clients and one of family and friends. To your clients, you'll need to send out a pre-trip email outlining where you're going and what you plan to see and do (together with possible feature ideas and on-the-road contacts), while friends and family will appreciate an indication of where you'll be should they need to get in touch.

- ◆ Take the time to become familarised with tourist board contacts as these may prove invaluable in providing assistance to upcoming trips.

- ◆ Check the Foreign Office website for updates on travel advice and warnings. By setting up specific Google alerts or news website profiles it is easy to stay abreast of developments in regions of the world or individual locations.

❝ YOUR OPINION COUNTS

An Expert's View...

Arriving at hotel receptions throughout 2008, bikini and flip flops in wheelie case, I could have done with a splash of cold water – this was in the name of work.

My remit was as follows: review spas. And so I did. From the Mandarin Oriental in London's Knightsbridge, to the Thermal Römerbad in Austria, via Holm House in Penarth. I sauna-d in Sweden, was smeared in Dead Sea mud in Jordan, and sampled the whisky (purely for research purposes) in Gleneagles.

How can you do the same?

(a) Be in the right place at the right time. I was lucky to be working with the right people on the health section of telegraph.co.uk, but I had been at the paper undertaking less glamorous assignments for three years.

(b) Have a background in travel writing. I had written already about many trips I had taken under my own steam.

(c) Be confident that your opinion counts. You don't need special qualifications to judge things that matter to the reader, like good customer service.

(d) Network. Once you begin reviewing, let it be known to PRs.

Finally, there is such a thing as a bad review. Write it. Publish it. Be honest. Or the good reviews will mean nothing at all.

Frances Booth is an award-winning travel writer. From 2007–2008, she reviewed spas for telegraph.co.uk. She is a former Guardian Young Travel Journalist of the Year. She now writes for a number of travel publications and also works as a copywriter. (Visit: www.herearesomewords.com)

FEES

As the title of this book suggests, it is more than possible to make money from travel writing although for many people it will always be a passionate pastime that just about pays for itself. Very few writers manage to earn a living solely from travel writing. This is largely because the rate per article makes it necessary to secure a steady five commissions per month to earn the UK's average wage of around £25,000 pa. This is more than possible but, of course, most people aspire to earning the equivalent of other paid professions. In order to do this, the writer needs to be a sales wizard as well as a writer. But again, this combination of skills is possible. An income of £40,000 or more is achievable (many earn six figure sums) but requires the ability to multi-task – as with every small business.

Some of the most successful travel writers – other than the best-selling big-deal authors – are the so-called worker bees who apportion time to serious marketing offensives to seek out deals all over the globe. They manage their time with precision to project-manage all their writing assignments to ensure that every job pays. Without exception, they only accept press trips or plan travel on the basis that the time is adequately covered by paid commissions. So, on the basis that a five-day trip to France requires at least three commissions (allowing for writing time), they launch a marketing drive to make it happen. Should writing commissions not be forthcoming from newspapers and magazines, they look to other sources of income. This could be tourist board copy-writing, photo sales or tourism reports – basically, anything that is travel related and enables them to hit their structured targets.

Having these clearly-defined goals is the motivation writers need to make things happen. It allows them to calculate a financial shortfall, say, for the upcoming month and actively explore ways in which to fill the revenue gap. They refuse to subscribe to the 'there simply isn't enough work to go around' theory. They view the world as their workplace and strategically set about exploring publishing options. This gives them many thousands of potential outlets, from contract publishing houses in the US and travel writing in education work in Asia, to tourism reports for major high street banks and newspaper articles for regional newspapers all over the world.

Occasionally, though just occasionally, they'll battle it out for the prestige of a commission in a national newspaper. However, as these assignments often require excessive amounts of nurturing many income-aware travel writers turn their attention elsewhere. They don't seek the glory of a big-name writing credit. They simply want to do the job they love – and to see the world and sell the story.

To work on this basis, you'll need some spreadsheet software and a basic project management package. Start by calculating the annual earnings you realistically need to earn. Then work this back to a monthly revenue. Allow for tax, a pension and cash-flow cushion to soften the months when you're waiting for cheques to arrive. Build in social and family time (and any other non-working days you can foresee) in order to gauge your annual or monthly working potential. Divide your required annual income by your working potential to assess a maximum average daily rate. Then use the same calculations to assess your bottom line – this will provide you with a minimum daily rate in order to stay afloat.

In time, you'll be able to get a 'feel' for how long, say, a 1,000-word travel feature piece will take you to write. But initially, be generous in the time you allocate per job. Building in adequate retirement provision is essential – even if you're in your early 20s. Many freelance travel writers have failed to save for the years when they no longer want to travel and write at full pelt. To realise this well into your 50s or 60s can cause significant financial anxiety, so it is paramount to plan ahead – even in the early years when you're struggling to get a travel writing career off the ground.

❝ SEE THE WORLD, SELL THE STORY

An Expert's View . . .

So many people write 'What I Did on My Holidays', my grown-up gap year, and think complete strangers will pay money to read it. They piece together emails they sent home and think it's a book. I'm happy they enjoyed their trip, but a travel book needs a story – an interesting premise, a beginning to hook the reader, a entertaining and informative middle and a satisfying end. And it's easier to market if it's set in one destination. I look for exotic high-concept adventure – Lost in the Jungle, Champagne and Polar Bears – and aspirational, do-able European experiences such as A Chateau of One's Own, Narrowboat Dreams or Dawdling by the Danube. ❞

Jennifer Barclay is Editorial Director at Summersdale Publishers and the author of *Meeting Mr Kim: Or How I Went to Korea and Learned to Love Kimchi.* (Visit: www.summersdale.com, www.authorsites.co.uk/jenniferbarclay)

In the UK, pay varies enormously for travel writers from around £150 per 1,000 words to £500 per 1,000 words. Guidebook fees are calculated either on a flat-fee basis or through royalties. How much you earn for your piece in a newspaper or magazine will depend on a number of factors. If it's a national newspaper, you'll benefit from large commissioning budgets, while if it's a contract published hotel in-room magazine the rates may be lower. Some publishers pay different rates to their contributors, depending on the credentials of the writer and the numbers of years they've written for the title.

In recent years, organisations such as the British Guild of Travel Writers (BGTW) have proactively sought to demystify the rates of pay by encouraging members to reveal what they've been paid. Some commissioning editors are upfront about rates, others less so. But it always pays to have an honest and open discussion so that you know what's what right from the start. Even the lowest per thousand word rate shouldn't be discounted without scrutiny. You may find that you're asked to produce longer feature pieces for some of the smaller, independent titles making them a comparable option money-wise. You may also find that a contract publishing house can offer you work on a volume basis across many different travel titles – as well as monthly web content. So it pays to keep an open mind even if the rate, initially, seems paltry. For example, in 2009 a well known web-based travel guide offered £30 per 100-word article. The vast proportion of UK-based travel writers turned the work down, decrying the rates as 'laughable'. Yet those who looked into the project with greater depth realised that it was possible to write three £30 pieces an hour. They accepted commissions on a volume basis, earning up to £3,000 a piece for less than two weeks' work.

❝ BE BAD, IT'S GOOD

An Expert's View...

Ask any newspaper publisher: bad news sells papers. If a reporter comes up with a story that makes somebody squirm, he or she is in business. Good news can sell, but it's a different skill. There's a limit to how many kittens rescued from trees an editor has room for.

Guidebook writing and publishing are not as far removed from tabloid journalism as it might seem. The most compelling guidebooks are those that are both practical and blunt, both useful and cheeky. Look at the Rough Guides to Britain, and their very canny annual gimmick of trashing parts of the country: local and national press coverage assured. Humour is very handy. If you're not a naturally humorous writer, there's no shame in falling back on old jokes, proverbs or anecdotes. At The Good Holiday Cottage Guide, *readers loved the complaint we had from a reader from Romford, in Essex, who wrote (this is word for word) of a farm cottage: "The accommodation was fine, but I wouldn't go back. I hated the way the sheep kept staring at us, and I thought the lavatorial habits of the cattle were disgusting." That got us a prominent letter in* The Times *and a plug for the guide.*

The basic when-to-go and how-to-get-there information in guidebooks usually has *to be formulaic. Beyond that, if you're lucky, you're on your own. Keep things fresh, original and a bit challenging. It can be creative and fun – worth a lot of midnight oil.*

For most destinations, the supply of guidebooks exceeds demand. Finding a niche can, however, make for success. How about a 'Peace and Quiet' guide? This would be very much in keeping with current thinking in an increasingly fraught and noisy world.

Bryn Frank is the editor and publisher of the *Good Holiday Cottage Guide* (Swallow Press), now in its 26th annual edition. For several years he was responsible for a number of the tourist guides published by what is now Visit Britain (formerly the British Tourist Authority). He has written several travel books about the UK and contributed widely to magazines and newspapers. (Visit: www.goodcottageguide.com)

A surprising number of publishers and editors have a small budget for travel writers' expenses – it's not much but it is up for grabs. For example, if you spend just £5 on a CD and postage to send your photos for each article – it could easily cost you more than £300 per year. To maximise your income from travel writing it is paramount to avoid these small amounts eating into your profit. Ask the magazine, newspaper or guidebook editor you're working with if you can reclaim postage expenses – the answer is usually yes. Other than postage, few other expenses are covered so you'll need to negotiate ways to cover your costs for transport and accommodation with other sources.

In today's global marketplace, you are increasingly likely to work for overseas publishers and editors. Many will quote a per-word fee – usually in the local currency. Unlike the UK, it is commonplace to ask for expenses when working with the US. Basically, if you are new to that market, clarify everything in detail – there may be extra income available to you, but you won't know unless you ask. When working with foreign publishers, currency issues come into play. In these instances it is crucial to know your Argentine peso from your Singapore dollar to avoid agreeing to write for a pittance or turning down some lucrative work. Some of the most successful income-generating freelance travel writers keep a watchful eye on currency exchanges – actively targeting outlets in countries where they get the best return for their rate (see page 211).

Although very few travel writers feel sufficiently confident to negotiate fees, it is always worth a try. Of course, tact and diplomacy are key to any sensitive financial discussions. I always tread carefully because the last thing you want to do is jeopardise future work. An apologetic 'I don't suppose there's any more money in the kitty to round it up to...' Or 'I hate to ask, but is there any way you could stretch to . . .' is by far the best approach. By squeezing an extra 5% out of editors across the board you'll raise an additional £1,200 per annum (based on the average UK income).

DON'T BE CAUGHT BY THE WEB

An Expert's View . . .

Someone once said to me that unless I value my writing I can't expect anyone else to, but surely being paid a little money is better than no money at all? Well, with a growing number of internet travel websites asking travel writers for free content it is a question that crops up with frequency. As an emerging market for the wannabe travel writers, the internet is ripe for exploitation – rates of pay often fail to come close to print media although this may change over time. So, check that the website is professional and gives out the right message and that there is real pay on the table – it may be preferable to set up your own.

Raichel Phipps is a British-based freelance writer, researcher and IT consultant. She has been involved in projects for a number of UK publishers and broadcasters.

STAY AT HOME TRAVEL WRITING vs WRITING ON THE ROAD

Although this book primarily focuses on the travel writer keen to travel as much as possible, it is worthwhile noting that many successful travel writers rarely venture very far from home. Not every travel story demands long-haul, extended periods of journeying – in fact it is possible to earn a decent income as a travel writer without roaming much, if at all. Specialists in snappy round-up pieces are often desk-based travel writers who may have travelled extensively once but who now prefer to work on home soil. Other writers may concentrate on their local area, selecting familiar subjects that are within easy reach in the town, county or region in which they live. Indeed, residence alone can be a worthy credential as a travel writer – many editors will seek a local writer with this expertise.

Benefits of travel writing without the need to roam far are obvious – it's less demanding in terms of time and therefore places less of a strain on finances or home life. It can also be a wonderfully rewarding experience to write about what you hold so dear you've made it your home. As a resident, you may also have unrivalled contacts and local insight that give you the edge on angles, content and expertise.

Almost every region will have a local magazine or newspaper with a domestic travel section while national outlets may want to feature your locality once or twice a year. Travel guidebook publishers always prefer to engage a locally-based author, while travel websites and portals require dynamic copy that is bang up to date from a person who is best placed to know what's what.

Other outlets include specialist publications, so it is important to get to the heart of your locality to understand how it can link to these, for example, camping and caravanning, golfing holidays, nature walking or yoga retreats. Should you live close to an airport, you may be able to write for a passenger magazine for an airport operator or a business travel or in-flight title. It may also increase your chances of writing a news peg piece based on events linked to luggage handling, industrial disputes and the opening of new terminals or runways.

Of course, writing about home soil can have its limitations, especially if it doesn't offer up a treasure trove of potential stories. For a writer with wanderlust, it can also be frustrating to stick so close to home while colleagues delve into the exotic and unknown. However, a good travel story can often lurk behind the most innocuous local landmark, myth or tradition – and, by utilising good powers of observation and applying strong research skills, a writer can bring this to life in a way that offers universal appeal. From a money-making perspective, working locally can also be financially rewarding because without the distractions and demands of travel, writers have a greater number of potential days per month to write – without the expense of overseas travel.

❛ A NICHE IS NICE

An Expert's View...

I believe that, to become a successful travel writer, you need a number of attributes: a thick skin, patience, flexibility and luck are but some.

I started writing through my photography as I was given an early tip that put me on the right track. Basically, I was told that by offering a complete package of words and images I could benefit – and it was sound advice. So, I began writing in order to give the photographs I was producing a better chance of being published – and it has served me well.

However, for most of us it is difficult to make a living entirely from travel writing so today I combine commissioned commercial photographic work with travel writing and photography. I spend a lot of time researching the market in order to come up with sellable ideas and to understand what is current. There are hundreds of potential publications to pitch to across the world, from obscure industry and in-flight publications to glossy travel magazines with household names. Some of my most profitable relationships exist with editors in English-speaking foreign countries. After seven years I have found a niche and I am enjoying the benefits of specialism – it is beginning to get editors phoning, writing and emailing me!

Richard Human is a freelance travel photographer, writer and guidebook author. (Visit: www.richardhuman.com)

2

How to Get Started

Like all great travellers, I have seen more than I remember, and remember more than I have seen.

Benjamin Disraeli

WRITING TO YOUR STRENGTHS

Writing is fulfilling in and of itself. Yet writers who want to earn money from their craft ultimately yearn to be successful in commercial terms – even if they don't reach the dizzying heights of Bill Bryson and Paul Theroux. Many writers starting out will find it easier to be prolific when writing to their strengths. Of course, good writers may also rise to the challenges of facing their creative weaknesses – but that can come with time. Initially, rather than struggle with the demands of a blank page, a preferable approach is to use what comes naturally – it beats sitting and staring at a computer screen all day.

Creating a positive mindset

A crucial component of the formula to achieving success is an ability to create a positive writer's mindset. Knowing that you are producing work of publishable quality is key, so be sure to assess all potential material with laser-focused intention. Ask yourself, does your knowledge of the subject give you the enviable insight to write about it with the seemingly effortless ease that not only engages a reader but offers them lots of insider surprises? Writing like this allows your creativity to roam. Feeling comfortable with a topic offers a wealth of possibilities as a writer and allows the confident use of personal anecdotes and a clever play on words. These, mixed with a delicate tone of light authority, enable a writer to deliver facts and information in a style that strikes an immediate chord with the reader. They trust, they engage, they imagine.

Doubts and insecurities are often all that stand in the way of publishing success. Many writers make an inventory of their beliefs about writing in a bid to eradicate, or at least identify, any negative feelings they harbour about their ability or strengths. By focusing on positive aspects and writing to your strengths it is possible to clear a more confident path on which to proceed. This greater self-assuredness will add untold confidence to the way in which you write. Never underestimate the importance of identifying what it is you should be writing about – a subject tackled with well-managed enthusiasm and self-belief is much more likely to win out.

Choosing subjects

To decide which subjects to focus on it may help to use visualisation in order to conjure up the potential look and feel of a piece of travel writing. Keeping this at the forefront of your mind can help clarify which elements should take precedence in the article. If you're a journal writer, then use your available resources to identify salient points, eye-catching headings or pull-out quotations and comment. Play around with a few ideas in relation to your chosen subject or angle and begin to flesh out a draft structure of your piece. Research is invaluable, be it to back up a hunch that an idea is timely or pertinent or to check that it hasn't been done to death already. Another good discipline is to brainstorm for words, phrases, potential content and recollections – you'll find that a full page of material can emerge organically simply by list making.

Chuck everything you conjure up into the mix – you can always sift through it later. Allow ideas to flow freely as you jot everything down to encourage one catchy word or phrase to lead to another. By galvanising the intention (what to write and why) and honing positive beliefs (I know this and I can do this), a writer is better placed to maximise talent and ideas to the full.

Journals are often invaluable in reassuring writers that they have the basis for a good travel piece – as a tool, they also enhance an ability to observe. Many of the best travel writers in the world are notable for their keen, clever, well-conveyed observations. Journals can also help mine emotions and thoughts in travel terms. When I flick through my own scribbled notes, I'm often staggered by the untapped potential they reveal in the imagery and colour they evoke. By penning my observations, I am giving my creative mind a regular work-out to muster up a flow of words – often in the least inspiring of places. This limbering up is a good test of detail – even when you know a place or subject well. It is also an essential tool when adding new material, while expanding your descriptive skills to keep a subject exciting and fresh.

For example, you may know Florence well – having walked every street and enjoyed extended stays in its handsome storeyed plazas. You may have absorbed all manner of minute detail, from its art history to its chichi boutiques and cafes. You may also have met a wide variety of local characters and enjoyed several successive journeys along the River Arno and made merry at its numerous historical festivals and events. Yet, as you sit in Piazza della Signoria, survey the scene – not in its broadest sense but by seeking out examples of the essence of the city, or something that reflects the 'here and now'.

Study the man and a woman sitting on a bench in the plaza to take in the possibilities as a writer. Around them, there are crowds of vendors engaged in noisy street haggling as street musicians serenade delighted tourists, sending pigeons scattering in alarm. Yet the couple sit, eyes locked and fingertips touching, oblivious to the melee. This single snapshot provides at least two possibilities: action and colour, or hustle and bustle if you choose the crowds. Yet Florence's romance could be focused on the sensual touching of fingertips under the ornate frescoes and gentle musical refrains of a strolling maestro. This is a useful skill to develop as it maximises the commercial possibility of your knowledge. For example, your knowledge of Florence could be invaluable in a destination piece but could also be used for specific outlets, such as honeymoon magazines, special interest magazines and round-ups that draw on the contrasting character of a place.

Being selective

However, there is rarely a need to describe everything in a scene in great detail – so a journal is rarely used in full. Throwing everything in simply bogs down the writing, so it is important to learn how to be selective – a great skill is using detail sparingly yet conveying it well. Writers who truly know their subject are best placed to know what to include and what to leave out. Detail-heavy prose can often highlight a lack of real personal insight. Write in a way that grabs and holds a reader – what you say should mesmerise and inform but never deluge. This is often achieved by using short phrases, good rhythm and well thought out awareness and pace. Remain mindful that you are writing for the reader – so stick to a plan (not easy, as many creative people have a tendency to resist structure) and shy away from using your writing as a showcase for *all* that you know.

Getting feedback

Writers who aren't sure of their strengths or weaknesses may find the feedback they receive from people who read their work useful. Are there any consistencies? For example, are you told that your settings are very descriptive and imaginative? If that is the case, your strength may be in this aspect. If the feedback is critical in some respect don't write it off as negative: weaknesses can often be things that a writer isn't sure of, for example conveying information without using first-person narratives.

By understanding strengths and weaknesses, a writer can better maximise what they do well. Few of us feel comfortable tackling something that might explode in our faces, so it is only natural to stick with what you know. The only way to improve upon weaknesses is to write them away.

Sometimes we need guidance on what we're doing wrong and perhaps even why it's wrong, though advice will only work when combined with writing practice. Writers may also be able to avoid weak areas all together – a tactic that only works if a weakness isn't something fundamental. If it is, you'll need to address this (see page 40) in order to progress.

Focusing on strengths and weaknesses

Writers who are keen to sell their travel writing should consider the following tips in relation to strengths and weaknesses. If you feel that your writing is missing something, but you're just not sure what it is, you'll need to identify weak areas. By focusing on strengths and working on weaknesses, your writing will be more complete – and ultimately, more sellable.

◆ Are you comfortable with your subject? Check that you have chosen it for the right reasons – it make well be in vogue and sexy but is it 'you'? Your writing will be much more confident if you truly know your stuff, so be sure that you are writing to your strengths – not your ego. Consider a destination you have travelled extensively or an event, such as an annual festival, you know well.

◆ Use travel notes and journals to back up your strengths – not only are they an invaluable source of information but writing them is a good discipline in observation and research. Using your own unique notes can bring untold confidence to a writer – and this self-assuredness will translate into writing buoyed by self-belief (see Take Note! on page 42).

◆ Is your chosen subject 'marketable' – is there a hunger for it somewhere? This doesn't necessarily mean that you need to ignore the obscure in favour of mainstream topics, but it will pay to do plenty of research in order to identify potential outlets.

◆ Have you identified your weaknesses and strengths? Be prepared to self-evaluate or call on others for a critique.

◆ Write a rough writing plan and utilise journals and online resources. Your writing plan should be an outline of the structure and content of your piece. Consider the following:

– First, formulate your ideas to ensure that the structure of your article is logical and appropriate to the subject and the outlet. For example, a consumer travel piece for a women's magazine is usually around 1,000 words so there is little point in crafting a 3,000-word travel essay.

– Keep it brief to remind you of important points that should be covered. Use headings to highlight the structure and pace of the article.

– Incorporate a notes section to add points to ponder or research. This is also useful if there is a choice of options to include or details to double check.

– Should you identify many different approaches to writing on one subject be sure to write them all down. Then save a copy of your plan together with a list of possible angles – this may well come in useful in the future, should you be commissioned to write on the subject again.

– Try not to put too much detail into the plan: use keywords and phrases, make notes of important references and species names that should be included. The purpose of the plan is to serve as your reminder of content to include and aspects such as introduction, order and rhythm.

◆ Put a draft structure together and honestly assess the following:

– Can you hook the reader in with good opening lines that capture their attention?

– Does your writing make a reader want to know more?

– How are you going to bond and engage the reader? Consider using surprise, evocative description, a unique character, emotion, witty dialogue, humour or a tale of the unexpected – or 'siding' with the reader in some way to nurture a sense of identification.

–   Will your writing set the scene? Consider ways in which your
    article will contain enough descriptive phrases and imagery
    for the reader to visualise the subject.
–   How will you pick up the pace? Be mindful that too much
    detail can slow down a story and deluge the reader. Use
    description sparingly and don't be afraid of skipping
    unnecessary details. Write the essential parts and let the
    reader's imagination fill in the gaps, using rhythm to up the
    flow.
–   Stuck for words? Brainstorm! You'll be surprised how a list
    of potential content, recalled events, words and snappy
    phrases soon turns into several pages – an invaluable part of
    the planning.
–   Set aside time for fact checking – the process of checking
    facts can help to decide which details should be included and
    which should be skipped.

⸂ TAKE NOTE!

An Expert's View...

*Trust me, very few good travel writers can rely on their memory.
Mine, for example, does such a good job of filtering out that I am
left with an amalgamated mass of confused recollections
punctuated by a few, crisp, clear encounters. I travel pretty much
year-round, often to new places, where the sensations can be
overwhelming. My notebook is my memory and I write everything
down – without fail. I favour a soft-covered, durable, pocket-sized
pad that is easily rolled up and stuffed in a rucksack. One way or
another I tend to use 95% of my notes in due course – often across a
number of very different articles. On some pages I scribble diary-
like, while other notes are a series of research memory-joggers
(such as 'big, brooding volcano in the distance – find out name and*

history') and random words ('HUGE!' or 'Green' or 'chaotic') and one-line phrases ('sea is at least seven shades of blue and there are sharks teeth in the sand'). When I review my journals I'm often truly astounded by what my brain has failed to recall – I mean, you'd think it would be impossible not to remember a place where garden furniture nailed to a horsedrawn cart constitutes a taxi. That's why a travel journal or notebook is an essential tool to every travel writer – you simply don't remember it all.

Sometimes, I use two notebooks – one for practical lists (bus times, prices and what I've photographed) and others for observations and impressions. But these often become merged into one when I'm reaching into my bag and forget which one is which. No matter, the important thing is to write things down so how or what on isn't the issue. Nothing should wait 'until later' – you have to do it then and there when your memory is fresh. Anything I hear, smell, touch and taste goes into my journal. All of these can make an article come alive to a reader – they are what makes your take on a place truly unique.

Sarah Woods (www.sarahwoods.co.uk)

FINDING YOUR NICHE

Having ascertained your strengths, the next step is to study the market in order to evaluate its plentiful bounty of potential outlets. Today's publishing world offers a growing array of possibilities for travel writers but it is important to research what's out there – and what is right for you. Obtain the full gamut of magazines and newspapers that appeal to you (buy several issues if you can) and print off a variety of extracts from online publications that catch your eye.

By conducting a full and careful analysis, you'll be able to gauge tone and style. This exercise will also highlight the type of subjects an outlet features on a regular basis as well as providing insight into word counts and focus. If the writing style, subject matter and tone strike a chord – then this could well be a niche for you. If not, continue this important background research until you have a 'hit list' of publishing possibilities that mirror your strengths, interests and style.

Writing on a variety of subjects
To make a decent living as a travel writer, you need to develop an ability to write about a wide variety of subjects. However, finding your professional niche within as broad a scope as possible will equip you with an area of expertise, without narrowing down opportunities. For example, an expert on travelling the Caribbean is able to cover backpacking, honeymooning, emerging markets and business travel.

While an expert on honeymooning could write about a wide array of European cities, isles in the Indian Ocean, round-up articles (Essential Packing for Romantic Rome) and industry trends from this particular perspective. By establishing a professional niche, you are more likely to be called on for expert comment and awarded commissions that require expertise. Of course it is possible to market yourself as multi-talented writer with multiple niches – within reason. A good example is a writer who has travelled extensively in Central and South America but who also knows golf travel inside out and is a frequent cruise passenger.

Niches can alter over time as they are impacted on by a writer's changes in lifestyle, beliefs, interests and, to a large degree, world events and trends. Travel guidebook authors are often considered authorities in the particular countries they write about, from its landscapes and people to its politics and cultures. Becoming an expert brings many writers greater freedom and, in turn, greater financial rewards as to write about something they know well requires less leg-work – leaving more time to develop their outlets and market their expertise. They are also more likely to be offered vehicles for self-promotion, such as providing expert-comment radio shows and TV broadcasts.

Monitoring travel trends

Monitoring travel trends in order to fully familiarise yourself with current markets and emerging story ideas is an invaluable aid to gathering potential feature angles. Consider 'objective travel trends' (which is all the rage right now when it comes to traveller behaviours and destinations all over the world) be it a rise in the number of Americans holidaying on home soil or a surge in Australians hiking in Hawaii.

Think ahead – what could impact on these trends? Consider a nation's major tourism campaign or a global sporting event and gather ideas ahead of the spotlight – both travellers and editors will be keen to exploit the opportunity emerging trends present. Scouring the travel sections, tourism marketing websites and travel trade publications will give you a feel for what is up-coming. Study tourist board facts and figures and resources such as the Foreign Office, World Health Organisation and National Statistics websites to identify an Objective Travel Trend – and with a bit of flair and research this can easily become a nucleus to a story. For example, how Colombia's falling crime rate has spawned a global tourism drive with tourist numbers predicted to double in less than five years.

'Editorial travel trends' are all about the amount of coverage afforded to a subject. For example, a conscious shift towards regular features for disabled travellers or a greater propensity to cover exotic weekend breaks.

'Subjective travel trends' are guided by anecdotal evidence and may lead to stories of how tourists who usually consider Spain are now looking to Latin America or how Panama City is the 'new Miami'.

ENHANCING YOUR SKILLS

Courses and workshops

Not only do courses and workshops help to expand the skill-set of a travel writer but they can also help to give confidence levels a much-needed boost. Guidance, tips and training can be invaluable in galvanising the motivation of a new travel writer, while even those with experience can benefit from the professional recharging a good course can bring. Good creative-writing instructors guide students through a journey of self-discovery whilst nudging them towards professional standards. The job is part cheerleading, part diagnostics and a large measure of explanation. A tutor should respect each student's ambitions and personal style whilst offering plenty of practical advice and feedback.

The vast majority of workshops and courses are for creative writing and offer travel writing as a specific aspect of their content. However, an increasing number of independent organisations now specialise in travel writing as a genre – some, such as Creative Escapes and Travellers' Tales (see page 255) even combine it with travel to an exotic location to offer the ultimate package.

A simple internet search will generate a large number of course options, from creative writing weekends and one-day workshops to ten days in Morocco or Spain. Some are part-government funded, others are fee-based and independently run by universities, community colleges, writers' circles, trade associations or privately-owned organisations.

Some of the best options are run by published travel writers with prospectuses that span all aspects of the craft, from drafting pitches to structuring a manuscript. These tend to engage a highly impressive bill of guest speakers and lecturers who understand the pressures and demands of the travel-writing world and convey advice based on first-hand experience.

An important component of travel-writing courses and workshops is how to deal with set-backs and rejection. Critiquing is also vital to fine-tuning and honing skills – so it pays to shop around to ensure the course you choose has good credentials and content that fully meets your needs.

Another useful skill to learn or improve is touch typing. Most community colleges run basic courses that take beginners to typing speeds of around 45 words per minute (wpm) – a useful addition to the skill-set of any travel writer keen to maximise efficiency.

Languages are extremely useful to any travel writer keen to roam the globe because they allow you to become more easily immersed in local culture through easy interaction and encounters. Of course, it is impossible for worldwide travellers to master every language and dialect – but Spanish and French are certainly useful for large areas of the globe, from the Caribbean and Africa to The Americas. Investing in phrase books and dictionaries is essential for travel writers exploring the globe – as they will reap the rewards of knowing the language basics to convey gratitude and greetings.

Familiarising yourself with social conventions and etiquette will also prove invaluable as they will help in avoiding potentially embarrassing faux pas. Writers planning to spend extended periods in unfamiliar locations may find it useful to attend privately-run courses organised by relocation agents and trade organisations. Content can range from basic orientation to how to do business and cultural tips.

❛ SPEAKING DA LINGO

An Expert's View...

For the intercontinental globe trotter, knowing a smattering of foreign languages can help them navigate some interesting cross-cultural challenges. Potentially enjoyable encounters can quickly turn sour over culturally insensitive actions or ill-chosen word or exchanges. Appreciating a country's linguistic nuances, their cultural protocol, customs and etiquette are all important in maximising your experiences and interactions. Swotting up on some simple local expressions can help avoid those potentially negative situations that leave a travel writer with egg on their face. It can help build better relationships and achieve goals and will highlight those direct literal translations and linguistic no-nos that ruffle feathers, bring down walls and make you a laughing stock. For example, it is hard to make a good impression as a worldly professional when you mistakenly inform the Spanish head of tourism that you want to bonk (as in make love) a bus when what I really meant was catch it. Then, having been told of my faux pas, I blushed and apologised profusely before inadvertently confusing my words once more. 'I'm so pregnant!' (Estoy muy embarazada!) I wailed, when what I meant to convey was my acute embarrassment.

Culturally, I have learned to have my business cards translated into Mandarin when travelling China; to welcome a dinner of whisky and red meat in Japan, and to know that a nodding head in Turkey actually means 'no'. My few words of Arabic have helped me no end, in Morocco, Egypt and the United Arab Emirates while managing to pull a few well-timed pleasantries out of the bag in Croatian has rewarded me with several friends for life.

Sarah Woods (www.sarahwoods.co.uk)

TOOLS OF THE TRADE

Travel writers 'on the road' generally rely on the following items:

- **Journal or notebook** (see pages 37 and 42). A 15 cm × 10 cm soft-covered, durable format often works best. Opt for stitched-in pages (because ring-bound spiral spines make packing problematic). Guard it with your life – because this is your memory. Write 'please return to:' with a clear note of a forwarding address (in English and the local language) in the event that it may be lost.

- **Camera**. Even if you're no David Bailey, a camera is a must as it can provide an important visual reminder of what you've seen – and where. Used in conjunction with your notes, a collection of memory-jogging photographs can add extra reminders of colours, location, ambience and detail – and can help transport you back to the place you're writing about. If you've an eye for photography, then developing this skill can be a financially rewarding add-on to your travel writing. Providing a magazine, travel guide or newspaper with a set of unique accompanying photographs with a feature article is a definite plus-point. It can often provide that extra push to publish your piece as you're offering a complete package. Sourcing images can often be expensive and time-consuming for a potential publisher, especially if the destination or event you are writing about is unusual or remote. Indeed some magazine editors, especially those with lower budgets, such as in-flight or member titles, are increasingly stipulating that images are required as part of the publishing deal. Guidebooks also tend to favour the author's own photographs.

It goes without saying that the better the photograph the more appealing it is – so it pays to work on your photography skills. Invest in a lightweight, compact digital camera and begin to build a portfolio of clearly labelled shots. Not only will a set of good accompanying images help to get your article published – it also has the potential to earn you extra money. So it is crucial to store your digital images in an easily retrievable format (there's no point building up a portfolio of 5,000 pictures if you forget where they are or what you've got). Create folders that cross reference, for example a photo of a coastal shot of a fisherman in Newcastle, Northern Ireland is relevant to 'Beach', 'Newcastle', 'Northern Ireland', 'Leisure' and 'Fishing'.

Consider investing in a tripod, zoom lens, Photoshop software and an external drive – all common tools of the trade. Most publishers will ask for high-resolution (over 300 dpi) shots at over 1MB each so it is best to use a digital SLR (single lens reflex) with six megapixels or more sensors. Traditional photographs, slides and transparencies are requested less and less in this digital age. Not only does digital photography avoid the high costs associated with development, but it also easier to store and manage (on CD or an external hard drive). Images can also be saved in low-resolution 'thumbnails' and sent by email to prospective publishers or burnt to CD in high-resolution format.

In order to take interesting, publishable photographs, it is important to think like an editor – what will illustrate the story, engage the reader and provide a compelling visual further insight to the subject. If the place is well known (and therefore much-photographed) take time to seek out interesting angles, colourful compositions and exciting perspectives to ensure a different take. Be aware of natural light (professionals favour just after sunrise and just before sunset) to ensure maximum colour and vibrancy. Choose subjects that illustrate the highlights and main points of your story or that capture the essence of a place, or a particular aspect of it. Play around with vertical and horizontal shots and the use of objects as a frame to ascertain what works – and what doesn't. You'll then need to be methodical in labelling each image clearly – it may help to keep a photo log in your journal.

Taking photographs for publication brings with it intricate legal considerations when it comes to people, logos and certain buildings and locations. Lonely Planet publishes a number of good, clear guides on this topic as do Lark Photography and National Geographic (also see Selling Your Snaps, page 55).

◆ **Laptop**. Travel writers keen to earn an income 'on the road' will need to stay in regular touch with editors, publishers and other potential clients. Don't rely on internet cafes as they may not always be open when you need them or exist at all in remote locations. With a laptop by their side, a travel writer keen to build up their client portfolio can pitch for ideas 'on the spot', follow up on ideas and strike while the iron is hot. By maintaining regular contact, a travel writer can appear to be 'at hand' wherever they are in the world. As strange as it may seem, it can be a source of great frustration for editors that travel writers actually travel – so by staying in touch distance and time differences can be minimised, allowing the writer to be a dependable contact in the event of last-minute commissions and queries. A laptop also allows the writer to pen articles as they go – ensuring minimal 'down time' when it comes to earning income. Images can also be downloaded instantly and deadlines met while 'on the road' with little, or no, interruption to your marketing efforts (see Chapter 3).

However, there are disadvantages to carrying an expensive piece of kit with you on your travels – from the worry of theft and the preoccupation of recharging laptop batteries to the inevitable wear-and-tear it will incur as you lug it around. Even the most robust model is unlikely to survive more than a year or two – so there is a clear cost implication. However, most travel writers – especially those determined to make a good living – will weigh up the expense of replacing a laptop against the benefits it brings when plying their trade as they roam. For example, it may cost £1,000 to buy a new laptop but without it you easily could lose more than that in lost income simply by being 'off the radar' and missing out on that all-important commission.

◆ **Mobile phone**. Invest in the latest technology to ensure you can be reached in every possible destination – even if your speciality subjects are relatively close at hand. As a travel writer, you'll never be sure exactly where your next job may take you – so it pays to be prepared. As mobile phone technology continues to evolve it is becoming increasingly easier for travel writers to stay in touch with editors and publishers to maximise potential income. Don't skimp on this aspect – simply factor in the cost as part of your overheads. If you intend to spend extended periods in a single destination, investigate local cell-phone deals and discounted tariffs. You can always circulate a temporary contact number as part of your on-going marketing – rental phones with pay-as-you-go pre-paid options can be surprisingly cheap.

◆ **Audio recorder**. Be it an old-fashioned microcassette recorder or high-tech minidisc or MP3, the audio recorder has long been the essential tool of the roving reporter. Choose a durable, hardy lightweight model that is easy to tuck into a pocket. Though many travel journalists still swear by the use of audio transcripts, the reality of play-back can be time-consuming and frustrating – so unless you intend to conduct interviews, it may not be for you. An audio recorder does, however, definitely come in handy when taking notes is simply impractical – such as on rough sea crossing or in a personal interview situation where you need to pay full attention to what your interviewee is saying. Much like photographs, an audio recording can also be used to capture the essence of a place or a situation – such as the evocative sounds of the deep, inner reaches of the Amazon jungle or an impromptu performance by a strolling Mariachi band on Mexico City's Plaza de la Constitution.

◆ **Other items**:

- – Currency convertor or calculator (unless your phone or laptop have this function and will always be at hand). This isn't just useful for keeping track of personal expenditure but is also vital for keeping business expenses in check too. As a global market, you'll also find that writing commissions are increasingly quoted in foreign currency – so it pays to be able to calculate the financial rewards of each job accurately, especially if you are weighing up one against another.

- – Batteries, solar rechargers, adapters, memory sticks, spare cables and power packs are essential if your equipment is a lesser-known brand or you're travelling off the beaten track (wrap them in waterproof plastic to protect them from humidity).

- – Work schedule. Be it in diary form or a simple list, you'll need an easily portable schedule of deadlines and start dates for on-going projects together with contact details (email addresses, fax and telephone numbers) and a brief/outline for each commission. You'll need to blank out suitable time to get the job done while you're travelling. Include invoice details and BACs transfer information to ensure you can start the ball rolling when it comes to being paid – wherever you are in the world.

RESEARCHING A STORY

Every travel writer approaches research differently, from undertaking vast amounts of pre-trip study to winging it until you're back on home soil. Much depends on how you're planning to write an article – if you've pitched the idea and been commissioned on this basis, it is likely that you'll have done some research already. If you've planned to travel as a source of material for a story, you may allow the requirements of research to unfold en route and supplement this with some post-trip study.

Most travel writers gather a wealth of research information as they travel, from the standard tourist leaflets and printed matter available in hotel lobbies to the detail available online. On the road, everything and everyone is a potential source of information – so it is essential to cultivate interaction with as wide a range of people as possible and keep a hold-all free for all the stuff you are likely to pick up along the way.

By keeping an open, curious mind and asking lots of questions you are more likely to return home with a variety of story ideas rather than a single option. Delve into every available aspect of a place to discover its potential – if you're short on time you can always research specific aspects later, but there is simply no substitute for spotting the extraordinary or lesser known rather than staunchly sticking to a lone, preconceived angle. Sure, have a focus – especially if you're travelling with a commission – but a travel writer keen to maximise their income will have their eye on all the possibilities. Consider every encounter in terms of its travel-writing potential, assessing it from different angles and for possible outlets in order to get to the seed of a story. Be sure to seize the opportunity to turn anything curious and compelling into another commission and, ultimately, cash.

❛ SELLING YOUR SNAPS

An Expert's View...

If you've an eye for photography and have captured some shots with money-making potential there are three main points to consider:

Agents: There are tons of very successful photographers with and without agents. Pros are they get you top quality work, charge proper rates and take the hassle of marketing your services out of your hands. Downside is they take 25% of your fee, which is clearly a lot, sell you into jobs you might not want to do, plus request you work solely for them. Plus the vast majority are fashion related with very few purely concerned with lifestyle/travel.

Cash: Like writers, photographers often have to wait ages to be paid. The larger the company the more hassle. I've waited four months for payment before and as a sole player in a saturated market, you don't want to start getting antsy (and they know it).

Recession: There is still tons of work out there. My advice is keep existing clients happy and regularly updated on what you are doing, for new clients work out new and interesting ways of making yourself known (sending a round robin email with a link to your site will just get lost or deleted). Call up, do some research on where they are at and call/get together face to face to explain. You're the expert, so give them some expertise. Works wonders. 〟

Jon Cunningham is a luxury travel and lifestyle photographer based in London. His work has been widely published in newspapers, magazine and coffee-table books around the globe, including *Daily Telegraph*, *The Guardian*, *Sunday Telegraph* and Rough Guides. He has photographed some of the world's finest hotels, including several Condé Nast *Hot List* and *Gold List*, *Design Hotels* and *Small Luxury Hotels of the World* members. He is currently working on his first solo photography book which is due to be published in July 2010.

SPREADING THE WORD

This book has touched on the importance of understanding what's going on in the travel-publishing world, and also aspects of self-promotion are highlighted to demonstrate the benefits of raising your profile in business and social circles. For more practical ways to market yourself and your writing, turn to Chapter 3. Meanwhile, as you consider establishing your travel-writing credentials, consider what you have to offer and what makes you special or different – it's a valuable exercise in defining your unique selling point (USP), which is covered in Chapter 4.

ACCOUNTING FOR SUCCESS

Knowing how you're faring financially as a business can often be an important motivating factor in thrusting you forward as a writer. Many travel writers have a strange fear of the unknown. Once they find a style that suits them, and a handful of outlets that like it, there is often a reluctance to look outside this comfort zone to seek out new potential clients. Knowing that you need to sell 20% more in order to hit a financial goal can often push a travel writer into trying something new. Fees vary enormously, so it is difficult to accurately forecast finances in terms of articles sold. However, by keeping accurate sales records and management reports, you'll be able to see how your sales and marketing efforts impact on your bottom line.

- Set up a sales record that details the total value of each commission as you get it. Include a note to remind you to pitch for add-ons, such as expenses or photograph sales.

- Set up an invoice record that correlates with the above, but that includes the client's payment terms – they can often be 60 days after publication, so it could be three or four months after you're commissioned. This record will allow you to manage cash flow.

- Put together a list of business overheads, for example, a monthly fee for an internet connection, mobile phone and professional memberships. Be sure to allow for sundries, on average, for example post, petrol, taxi fees and stationery.

- Create a monthly sales report (a summary of the sales record) that allows you to chart how you're doing month-on-month. Over time, this will clearly show your busiest periods and the months in which work is lighter – an important reference point when taking on new, big projects or deciding when to focus on a sales and marketing push. It will also allow you to predict your annual net and gross income, which is useful for tax planning purposes and expenditure decisions.

- Keep a list of reinvestment (new laptop and other essential items) possibilities in order to flag up likely upcoming expenditure. Also, a note of when memberships expire and of travel insurance renewals.

- Include an estimated percentage amount to allow for annual inflation and rises in the cost of living – you'll need this when determining next year's budget for the business.

- Search out commission-free currency deals, low-interest credit cards and banks that provide fee-free ATM withdrawals abroad. Investigate the benefits that come with any professional memberships you have – these often include discounted travel insurance, significant reductions on transport and good deals on medical products.

- Establish the VAT threshold (it may pay to earn under this amount) and clarify your tax obligations. On the basis that time is money, it may be cost-effective to engage an accountant rather than struggle with lengthy forms and questionnaires. An accountant will also be able to outline tax efficient expenditure. For example, you may be able to claim a mileage allowance for travel on a bicycle and purchase IT equipment favourably.

COMMUNICATING WHO YOU ARE

An important part of launching a travel writing career is telling everyone that you're a travel writer – a simple first step in self-promotion that can often lead to introductions and recommendations. Consider also joining writing circles, networking groups and travel writing associations in order to maximise contacts and sales opportunities. A good first step is to get some business cards printed (using a logo that is suitable for all your corporate ID needs) – you'll find that many social and business settings will offer an opportunity to tout for possible work. Practical marketing is covered in more detail in Chapter 4 when it considers the following options:

- mailshots;
- email bulletins;
- website;
- Twitter;
- Facebook;
- business cards;
- letterhead;
- logo (corporate ID).

❝ PROMOTING FOR SUCCESS

As soon as I made the decision to become a travel writer, I began introducing myself as such in business and social settings. Though a simple act of self-promotion, it immediately began to pay dividends. I would leave cocktail parties with scribbled names on napkins and useful introductions to editors and publishers. My plentiful stock of business cards includes contact details and my website address.

When I analyse website traffic there is a clear and obvious link to these individual events – I may well have spoken to only 25 people but visitor figures indicate a cascade effect with four times that amount of traffic. So far, I have gained commissions directly from speaking to my consultant during a hospital appointment, by chatting with a guy I was seated next to on a flight to Miami and from a chance encounter at a house-warming party in Andalusia. I consider myself a sales representative and publicity machine for my own enterprise.

As a travel writer, I view all encounters as (a) fodder for a potential story; and (b) an opportunity to explore work possibilities – it's an important two-pronged approach that helps me maximise my income and creative output.

Sarah Woods (www.sarahwoods.co.uk)

GETTING PUBLISHED

Having conducted your research you will be armed with a good list of various outlets that published travel articles along with the styles of writing they carry. You should also have an idea of what subjects or destinations are frequently covered, along with the formats that appear occasionally. These will normally be divided into long-haul and short-haul subjects with a target consumer traveller who ranges from shoestring to mainstream and luxury. Having trawled through archived material online you'll have ascertained which topics could be due for publication again. By keeping notes of these you will be able to refer to dates or timings – something that will demonstrate your commitment to research and save you from the embarrassment of pitching an idea that appeared a week ago.

Next, it is important to check out the contributor guidelines for all potential freelance submissions. Not only do these outline how editors prefer to be approached and when, but they also outline what styles of articles they will consider. It is pointless – and a great annoyance to commissioning editors – to send in pitches that don't meet the guidelines. By following them to the letter, you will immediately maximise your chances of being published. Of course, an even better way is to be introduced or recommended by a respected colleague who has already established a relationship with the publisher or editor. This is something you should work on developing through your marketing efforts (see Chapter 3) and spreading the word (page 56).

Newspapers

In the UK, newspapers range in style and format from the local weekly 'freesheet' newspapers (not sold but distributed free to households), to the 100 or so 'paid-for' local and regional newspapers that are published on a daily or weekly basis. Although some of these titles carry travel articles, much of the content is bought-in syndicated content, offering little opportunity for freelance submissions (there are some exceptions, so it does pay to do some research in order to establish commissioning potential).

The major outlet for travel writers is the high-profile 'national' newspapers as these boast the highest circulation – and therefore the highest budgets for freelance contributions. They also all carry some travel content, although this is scant in both the 'redtop' and 'middle' tabloid category of the UK press. At the quality end of the 'nationals', the broadsheet newspapers offer travel writers greater scope as their travel sections tend to be a weighty part of their make-up.

Every broadsheet has a Sunday equivalent title, staffed by a completely separate editorial team. Therefore, travel writing freelancers have two potential bites at the cherry as they are able to pitch ideas for the weekday and Saturday issues as well as the Sunday edition. Some of the travel supplements can be as large as 40 pages. Much of the content is written by freelance travel writers and is commissioned by a dedicated travel team. Some of the feature content is planned up to 12 months in advance in conjunction with the newspaper's advertising department.

Travel writers with good contacts are often able to gen-up on upcoming plans for a destination-specific supplement (such as Caribbean Island Special) or special pull-out (on, for example, Solo Travel) – valuable intelligence that allows them to make perfectly-targeted pitches to the travel desk that truly hit the mark.

It is easy to stereotype newspaper travel editors – and of course, each is very different with varying working styles and characteristics. However, what is common to each is that they are incredibly busy in a high-pressure environment. Most write (usually a weekly column and often a major feature), edit, manage staff and content, attend meetings and pull everything together via liaison with design, art, photography and the sales department. They also commission – but rarely have the time to seek out new talent, offer critique or spend time chatting with potential freelance contributors. National travel editors receive hundreds of pitches per week, many of them way off beam or without an obvious peg – and they rarely have time to study each one in great detail, so they scan through to see which ones work and which don't. What they expect from a travel writer is a piece that fits in with the style, tone and format of the title. If it does, then great – it stands a chance of being accepted. If it doesn't, it is consigned to the bin – it's as simple as that.

One of the least rewarding ways to attempt to get your work published is to write a piece and send it out of the blue. Unsolicited submissions arrive on the travel editor's desk without warning – so it would take an extraordinary combination of luck and fortitude for it to fit in with the editorial publishing schedule.

Given the 'off the radar' nature of a busy travel editor's working day, it is almost impossible to get any idea if it'll ever be used – or is one of the many tossed aside. It is only acceptable to submit an unsolicited article to one newspaper at a time – pitching this way is time-consuming and frustrating. It is also financially questionable, as you've incurred the costs of travel and writing the piece without any confirmed sales outlet.

A better explorative approach is to submit a piece 'on spec'. This is done after an editor expresses an interest in a pitched idea. It is not a confirmed commission, but neither is it a complete stab in the dark. If the editor likes the finished article, they'll publish it – but this all hangs on the final piece being up to scratch.

Pitches need to be specific, well thought out and with a clearly defined angle. It is not enough to ask if an editor is 'interested in a piece on Mexico' – you'll need to demonstrate that you know a subject well, have considered an interesting peg and understand the requirements of the readership. Most editors prefer to be emailed with submissions or proposals but some still favour approaches by post – so be sure to refer to the guidelines before you send your pitch. Only the very brave, or foolhardy, attempt to pitch by telephone – but those who do decide to call should avoid press day at all costs.

Ideas that are so well pitched and so well timed and targeted are commissioned – a guarantee that it will be run. This is the security that all freelance travel writers relish as it confirms payment and allows the writer to approach tourist boards, airlines, tour operators, car rental companies and hotels for assistance (press trips and free facilities) with putting together the trip that will support the piece.

❝ PAIRING UP WITH PRs

An Expert's View...

PR practitioners are constantly looking to persuade us travel writers to produce features and images for client destinations and travel pursuits worldwide. And no wonder. Editorial coverage is free and the independent endorsement of a place carries far greater weight.

Why is it, therefore, that PR people send us information which, while obviously pampering the client's ego, also seems destined to alienate the very people they are looking to influence?

We want key information in a no-frills format. We get glowing prose saturated in superlatives, hyperbole and irrelevances. If PR people saw the value in commissioning travel writers to source and prepare copy for their press releases, the upturn in interest would please the client, reward the agency and satisfy the travel writers.

And just think how more alluring holiday advertising and tourist brochures would be if we were given the chance to produce the copy.

We are approached by PR agencies all the time. Why not suggest a collaboration? It could bring real and mutual benefit.)

Ashley Gibbins is Director of the International Travel Writers Alliance and Managing Editor of *AllWays* – the consumer travel service from the Alliance. He also runs development workshops for travel writers, travel industry representatives and agencies with travel related clients. (Visit www.itwalliance.com and www.allwaystraveller.com)

Press trips

Press trips are usually organised excursions or group holidays specifically created for editors or travel writers. Most travel editors receive dozens of different press trips each week, from weekending in Yorkshire and camping in France to safaris in Kenya and island-hopping in Hawaii. Press trips have long been the mainstay of the travel-writing scene but can sometimes lack the flexibility and independence required to get a unique story. Because of this, a growing number of travel writers and editors arrange independent press trips without the restraints of a group. This avoids a potential problem with competing outlets vying for the same story and allows writers to tailor-make a trip that truly suits their story needs.

These free facilities are usually negotiated on a story-by-story basis on the understanding that the travel organisations that have stumped up will be fully credited within the piece. This publicity and promotion is the pay-off for the freebie – an accepted practice and commitment that the writer is expected to honour under the terms of the trip. Despite the business-class ticket or five-star luxury suite so often offered as part of a press trip deal, a good travel writer should be able to clearly demonstrate that they are able to remain objective.

No writer should feel compromised by freebies and it is important that a piece retains the integrity that a reader assumes is a given. Press trips often raise the question of impartiality and, understandably, the principles of some publications prohibit this type of perks-for-publicity trade-off. To by-pass the no-freebie rule, some organisations offer discounted press rates, thus making it affordable and acceptable for freelancers to make the trip. If the publication you are writing for, or pitching, clearly states it will not accept articles subsidised by press trips – it pays to be up-front and honest about discounts and press rates. It is all too easy to become embroiled in a tricky situation that could, ultimately, backfire and lose you future commissioned work.

A PRESSING MATTER

An Expert's View

At the Italian Tourist Board press office, we are interested in hearing from travel writers who are keen to write about any aspect of Italian culture, the landscape of Italy or its many tourist attractions. In return, we offer a wide range of aids and practical assistance to help equip the writer with facts, figures, details, images and feature-story suggestions. We are also able to arrange travel and accommodation for writers travelling to Italy, although this is assessed on a case-by-case basis depending on the scope of the project. What we need from the writer is a clear outline of the angle of the story they are writing; the details of their commission (outlet, circulation and publication date) and a rough idea of what they are looking for in assistance. During the course of the last three years, our London office has supported over 300 press trips to Italy, from cultural tours of Florence and city-breaks in Rome to wildlife treks in some of Italy's most scenic national parks. In return, Italy has appeared consistently in a wide range of media outlets, from regional and local newspapers and glossy lifestyle and consumer magazines to TV travel shows and the national press.

Alessandra Smith is a Press Officer at the Italian Tourist Board in London. (Visit: www.italiantouristboard.co.uk)

Magazines

Given that magazines are usually published monthly, bi-monthly, quarterly or bi-annually, it tends to be a less pressurised, frantic environment – unless there's a deadline in sight. Magazines fall into four main categories: specialist travel (specific, dedicated travel); lifestyle (niche magazines that include some travel content); trade (travel-specific trade topics) and corporate magazines (such as in-flight or cruise passenger titles).

In many ways, pitching to a UK magazine is very similar to submitting an idea to a newspaper (see page 63) in that it is preferable not to send unsolicited material. However, magazines have very different lead times to the newspaper industry – with much of the content commissioned several months in advance (feature lists can be scheduled 12 months ahead of publication).

To pitch appealing ideas to magazines, writers require an ability to look into the future in order to suggest timely articles and content of upcoming trends. Seasonal pieces will often see 'Where to Enjoy a Sun-Soaked Christmas' pieces tackled in July, while destination stories that explored Washington to coincide with Barack Obama's inauguration ceremony were penned in the days just after the votes were counted. Millions of different magazines contain travel content of one type or another, ensuring there are plenty of opportunities for travel writers. However contributor budgets vary dramatically so, as a consequence, rates do too. Unlike national newspaper pitching, it is acceptable to send simultaneous pitches to multiple magazine editors. However, each should be tailored to suit the style and tone of the individual publication.

It is also important not to pitch the same angle to competing titles. Like newspaper editors, most magazine editors prefer to receive pitches and story ideas by email. You're more likely to get noticed if you can name-check a freelance colleague you have in common or make an approach via recommendation – so try to secure this if you're able to.

PITCHING POINTS TO PONDER

Of course, every newspaper or magazine editor is different but every travel writer composing a pitch should consider the following points.

- Is it concise, logical and self-explanatory?

- Does it outline the specific angle, unique peg and relevance to the publication?

- Does it capture the colour, experience or ambience with clever use of evocative prose?

- Are the editor's name and magazine name spelt correctly?

- Have you checked the grammar and punctuation?

- Does the pitch conform to the contributor guidelines?

- Are you sending the pitch at a time it stands a chance to be read (e.g. not on deadline or press day)?

- ◆ Does the email contain details of how the editor can contact you?

- ◆ Have you included an URL to previously published work or a website address for the editor to find out more about you?

Given the global nature of travel writing, it is not uncommon for all commissioning to be conducted by email – though some editors may invite you to call to discuss the story outline in more detail. It is usual to receive a brief once you have accepted the commission. This is an outline of the structure, angle, tone, word count and deadline you have agreed. However, the scope and style of each brief varies dramatically depending on the publication, from a short email paragraph to a full three- or four-page document sent as an email attachment. Larger publishing organisations will follow this up with a contract for signing and this will also detail the rights on which the story is being sold. They may also set up a BACS payment on their accounting system to ensure your fee reaches you automatically, in accordance with their terms and conditions (see Fees on pages 24–31). Otherwise your brief, or contract, will specify who to invoice and how – often with a purchase order to quote.

❛A SYMBIOTIC SOURCE

An Expert's View...

If you've a story angle it is worth talking to the respective public relations representative to brainstorm the options – but don't expect them to arrange a press trip until you have secured a definite commission. Exactly how much support is offered (in terms of flight, hotel, or ground arrangements) depends on the calibre of the publication you are writing for. The days of the total freebie are gone – so writers should be prepared to pay a media rate for part of the trip.

For one of my clients, Vale do Lobo in the Algarve (www.valedolobo.com), I set up around 20 media visits per year, provided that the journalist is definitely producing an article after the trip. We offer three nights complimentary accommodation for a writer (and a guest) plus a round of golf or spa treatments. In return, the resort usually gets a one- or two-page spread. However, flights are increasingly more difficult to offer on a complimentary basis.

I do get journalists contacting me who are planning a holiday to the Algarve. They ask for a free round of golf or other free extras at Vale do Lobo – but have no intention of writing anything afterwards. I politely tell them that we haven't got the budget to help (but inside I am thinking 'what a cheek'!) ❜

Vanessa Aves is an established travel and tourism PR and the founder of The PR Network. Tel: 01372 722476/Mobile: 07721 413358.

Press trips

Press trips (sometimes called media trips) are sponsored by a destination (sometimes a resort, at other times a tourist board or Chamber of Commerce) and are offered to people who work in the media (journalists, writers, reporters, bloggers, etc). Trips come in many forms but are usually open only to writers who meet certain criteria – the stringency of this varies but more often than not a commission, or the hope of one, is the crux.

Newish travel writers invited on their first press trip will find them an excellent way to network with PR contacts and other writers. By establishing good relations you'll almost certainly be invited on other press trips – as long as you come up with the goods in terms of coverage. To appear like a seasoned pro, be sure to consider the following in preparation before your trip – it will help no end.

- Do your homework before you go: research the destination online and read everything you can find. Create a list of questions before you go and take it with you. If you've been commissioned, jot down a few notes to help you meet the brief during your trip.

- Pack a good quality digital still camera to help record the places you visit – they'll be useful reminders when it comes to writing when you get home. You may also be able to sell them with your piece.

- Update your Twitter account, Facebook and MySpace during your trip to let clients know what you are doing. Do this in conjunction with an email bulletin that should highlight the specifics in detail.

- Make a good impression and take advantage of any time you get to spend with tourism officials and resort management – as you'll never know when you'll get to meet them again. Ask plenty of questions and get some official answers and be sure to exchange business cards and contacts.

- Take advantage of any activities offered to you as part of your trip – they've been laid on for a reason, so try to put your personal likes and dislikes to one side.

- Sample as much of the food as you can – ask your PR contact to point you in the right direction for a taste of the local dish or drink.

- Maximise all the local contacts you meet who are really 'plugged in' to the local scene – ask them to keep you abreast of local happenings and events and urge them to stay in touch.

- Speak to other guests and holidaymakers about their experiences – you may get alternative ideas for a story or get some great quotes and comments for future pieces.

- Remember that you aren't 'on vacation' so ensure that you behave accordingly. Dress appropriately, be punctual and be sure to personally meet all your sponsors and trip organisers. Follow the example of the press trip leader in style, tone and behaviour – even if the sun is shining and the booze free-flowing.

- Do not fail to make notes about every aspect of your trip – it will help you sell different angles to various outlets. Pick up brochures and gather research with as wide a scope as possible.

- Be sure to network with your peers as you never know where friendships and collaborations may take you. It is possible that one may be a potential client one day, so view every encounter as such – and make it count.

- On your return, always follow up with a 'thank you' to the press trip sponsors and organisers. Extend this courtesy to anyone else who helped along the way, from tour guides to transport companies.

- Stay in touch with sponsors and organisers to provide them with links to your articles, photos and online reviews. Without this, press trip sponsors and organisers won't know the part you played in raising awareness of their product, so you may not be invited again.

Books

Travel narratives

Generally speaking, there are two ways to secure a publishing deal for a book-length travel narrative – but the commonest is to approach a publisher with a synopsis together with two or three sample chapters. This is often enough to gauge publisher interest. However, if you have written the book in full, it may pay to send the whole manuscript in order to maximise the impact of the story.

A book proposal is an extended pitch that summarises the theme, structure and content of the story. It may require a paragraph on the background and origin and it will certainly stand a better chance of being successful if it outlines why the subject is a compelling must-read. Some facts, statistics and justifications are a common inclusion – for example, why it should be published, who will read it, why they will read it, and why it is timely to publish it now. Also make note of any other books on a similar theme – if it has sold well then the publisher will see a ready-made potential readership as long as the subject is being tackled from a different angle.

Of course, some lucky writers are able to secure a commission just from a suitably enticing pitch – although this is a rarity. If you can engage an agent, allow them to deal with the proposals on your behalf. Otherwise, approach the publisher direct (they may politely ask you to reapproach them when an agent has been engaged or may be happy to embark on the proposal direct).

If the idea is a hit, the publisher will ask you to sign a contract that commits you to an agreed deadline, advance (a fee paid upfront to you that is later recouped from subsequent book sales) and any other financial and legal obligations. Advance payments vary dramatically, depending on the size of the publisher and the distribution deals it has in place. However, in most instances it is enough to cover the expenses you incur whilst researching the story and to provide a financial cushion while you work on the project. Smaller, independent publishers will offer a lower advance payment based on what it anticipates it can realistically sell without the full might of a slick, well-oiled marketing machine and global distribution network. Financially, this may be a disappointment – but the project may still well be worth accepting on the basis that it may lead to future work.

Once you have accepted the commission, the commissioning editor hands you over to an editor whose job it is to guide you through the manuscript stage to final publication. The editor assigned to you is part task-master and part-champion; the force that drives you through the hard work of producing a publishable manuscript and marketable final product. You are likely to love and loathe your editor in equal measure as they alternate between delivering strong, loyal support to coaxing you to pull your finger out and pushing you on and on. Ultimately, you are both aiming for the same thing – a book to be proud of. It pays to combine forces harmoniously and work together with a shared common goal to iron out glitches and give weak areas a tweak.

❛ KNOW YOUR STUFF

An Expert's View...

In my commissioning role, the main thing I am looking for in the first instance is a thorough knowledge of the destination and recent travel experience there. I have known writers who have tried to 'wing' a piece using internet research and a long-forgotten trip, but really, editors can tell when someone is writing about a place they have not been to or don't know very well!

Following the brief is crucial, too. We have a very strong idea of what we want, in terms of content and style. When a writer doesn't follow the guidelines provided it is very frustrating – invariably the text will go back to the writer immediately for revision, which can be stressful for both parties when deadlines are looming. DK Travel has a strong list with both established series and hugely successful one-off 'coffee-table' travel books, so if you are pitching a new title for us, it is wise to do your research first. Is the destination truly up-and-coming? Who are the competition for this type of book and is your idea really different enough to stand out from the crowds?

Sadie Smith has been working in illustrated book publishing for 14 years, moving over from children's reference to travel guides in 2004. In 2006, she became a Senior Editor for DK Travel to look after the Top 10 series of guides (2009 Winner of Wanderlust Travel Gold Award – Best Guidebook Series). (Visit: www.traveldk.com)

Travel guidebooks

There is absolutely no point in producing a manuscript for a travel guidebook without a commission. Researching a guidebook is extremely time consuming and, given the time-sensitivity of the data, it needs to be published without delay. Most guidebook authors are travel writers who intend to spend an extended period in a country they know well – often their country of origin or second home. To pitch a guidebook idea, you must first consult the publisher's guidelines for submission. It is also imperative to check their current portfolio of guidebook titles to avoid pitching a guide that is a long-standing existing best-seller.

Not all guidebook publishers are the same, each specialises for a slightly different type of traveller. This may be the backpacker, older adventurer, family traveller or culture seeker – and your pitch should mirror this. By doing plenty of research on why a specific guide should be published you need to be able to produce a brief commercial justification for the project. This highlights why the time is right to produce this guide. For example, your pitch might cover the following points.

◆ Will World Cup football or a new Easyjet route bring an increased tourist demand, or are visitor figures up two-fold on the previous year?

◆ What is the competition (are there other guides and if so when were they last updated – and how will yours be different?).

◆ What does the tourist board predict next year's visitor figures will be (and do these stack up according to trend?).

Include your own credentials (this should clearly convey why you are the best person for this specific job), together with any support material that support your proposal (CV, writing samples, etc).

Be sure to tailor your pitch to the individual publisher – there is little point pitching a great guide to shoestring travel around Costa Rica if the publisher specialises in luxury guides to European cities.

Once you've been commissioned, a contract will be sent to you in which the terms and fees for the project are confirmed. Most travel guidebook publishers pay a small advance to cover flights and some basic expenses – but if you are planning to spend six months gathering material in the subject destination the payment is likely to fall short of covering the cost. Travel guidebook writing has a reputation for being poorly paid but, in truth, a good travel writer undertaking guidebook writing should be able to secure additional commissions from a variety of outlets to run concurrently (see Stacking up the Costs on page 78).

Guidebook authors also have a golden opportunity to amass saleable photographs as they journey the length and breadth of a nation. This should be managed as part of the pre-trip preparation so that when you leave the UK you have a confirmed base of commissions to top-up the income from the trip. Once the guidebook is published, the author is usually paid royalties according to sales – the details of which will vary from publisher to publisher but are outlined in the contract. Other publishers work on a flat-fee basis, generally offering a lump sum divided into staged payments over the different phases of the project – the signing of contract, submission of the manuscript, proofing and sign-off.

Whether you are paid on a fee or royalty basis, as the author you will need to cover all the costs of your trip. It is therefore customary for authors to seek assistance from tourist boards, hotels, tour operators and airlines in return for inclusion in the guide – but on the basis of author impartiality. It also pays an author to maximise their contacts in order to secure help with gathering specific information, such as maps and transport schedules.

Guidebook writing is hard graft that requires an enormous amount of leg-work, from visiting hotels and restaurants to walking unmapped streets in order to produce a decent sketch of its layout. However, it can also be an incredibly rewarding project in which the author is established as an authority on the destination – leading to documentary work and further commissions.

STACKING UP THE COSTS

Assuming you need £750 to cover half the rent or mortgage on a house (plus bills) the following cost calculations demonstrate how a project-managed guidebook research trip can cover costs. By adding consultancy fees for documentary work, location scouting for film production companies or copy-writing for the PR company or major tour operators that cover the destination – you will be in a profit-making situation. Strictly speaking, your guidebook work could be restricted to the 60 'working days' that make up three months, allowing 24 days for potential other income-paying projects.

- Number of days travelling – 90.

- Outlay (assuming flights, accommodation and ground transport is sponsored) – £150 for kit, medicines, etc.

- Daily expenses × 90 days at £25 per day = £2,250.

- Total income required to cover 90 days' costs at home – £2,250 + outlay (£150) = £2,400.

- £2,400 + £2,250 = £4,650 (total amount to cover costs).

- 5 × commissions per month (at average of £300 each) = £1,500.

- Sundry works, such as public speaking events (bookshops, tourist board, embassy and tour operators) – or web-guide updating, attendance fee for one engagement and payment for one day updating = total £150.

♦ This equals £4,650 (based on 70 days' work on the guidebook and 20 days on income-generating work 'on the road'). Reduce this to 60 days on the guidebook and 30 days on income-generating work (based on ten days of sundry work + 5 additional commissions) = £2,250 + £3,845 = profit of £1,445.

❛BOOK AHEAD!

An Expert's View...

As a commissioning editor, like everyone else in book publishing and particularly in travel publishing, I'm under considerable time, budgetary and commercial pressures. My job is to come up with new projects, recruit authors and act as the main point of contact with authors. Book ideas come from the commissioning editor themselves, from authors, or a combination of the two.

By following the rules below, travel writers stand a better chance of being commissioned, when they contact commissioning editors like me:

1. *Do your homework – only contact relevant publishers and find out the name of the appropriate commissioning editor.*

2. *Post* and *email your pitch. Keep it professional, simple and to the point. This is not 'your baby', this is a business proposal. Include a portfolio and short sample material.*

3. *Present yourself as an expert in a country or travel theme – don't say that you can write about anything (even if you can).*

4. *Demonstrate that your book is commercially viable. Where would it fit into the travel book market? What makes it different from other books? Who would buy it?*

5. *Follow up with a polite phone call and quickly talk them through your pitch.*

6. *Be flexible and open to changing your book concept to fit the needs of the publisher and their commercial imperatives. Don't be precious about your vision for the book.*

7. *Do negotiate your fee/advance, but also be realistic. Travel writing is not well paid.*

8. *Never make demands regarding the book or cover design.*

9. *Be a dependable and hassle-free author. Deliver on time, on budget and on brief and you may well be commissioned again and again.*

Ross Hilton has edited travel guides for Compass Guides and Bradt and was formerly a commissioning editor for travel books at New Holland Publishers and Cadogan Guides. He is now a freelance commissioning editor and travel writer. (Contact Ross Hilton at: editor@rosshilton.co.uk)

3

Boosting Sales

MARKETING FOR SUCCESS

Being able to anticipate trends is a valuable skill for a travel
writer who is keen to fill their schedule with advance commissions.
For example, numerous guidebook publishers commissioned new
titles about Beijing once the host nation of the Olympics 2008 was
announced – rewarding the many travel writers who, with
foresight, pitched their ideas and credentials early on. Ahead of
the Caribbean World Cup cricket tournament in 2007, several
travel-related articles were published as a 'peg' to the speculation
about what increased tourism to the region would bring. Every
travel writer keen to maximise their income should devote time to
analysing their potential outlets – as well as their competition.
This basic commercial principle has been the mainstay of
achieving a competitive cutting edge for centuries – and it applies
to travel writing, just as it does to any other business sector.

BUSINESS-MINDED PROFESSIONALISM IS KEY

An Expert's View . . .

*To be a successful travel writer, you need to be proactive,
professional, and a pleasure to deal with. It's no good being a
prima donna over copy changes or last-minute alterations to your*

brief, just as it never pays to kick up a huge fuss on a hosted press trip. Stand up for yourself – but always take the polite route first. Word quickly gets round about which writers are good to deal with. Make sure you are one of them.

Editors want freelances who can consistently come up with good ideas; who can provide quality copy to deadline; but who are easy to get along with too. Aim to establish yourself as a regular contributor in several non-competitive publications by feeding a steady stream of carefully targeted ideas – not forgetting you'll probably need to provide your own images or at least a reliable source. And always look 12 months ahead, so you can work on seasonal features at the right time. Then all you have to do is deliver, preferably ahead of deadline in case there are queries. Simple really! ”

After writing everything from parenting features to celebrity interviews and countryside articles to corporate copy, Gillian Thornton became a full-time travel writer in 1997. A member of the British Guild of Travel Writers and Travelwriters UK, she now specialises in France. Gillian writes features for both francophile and general interest magazines, as well as brochures for French regional tourist boards. (Visit: www.travelwriters.co.uk/gillianthornton)

Market research

Market research generally falls into two categories: consumer market research and business-to-business (B2B) market research. Consumer market research studies the buying habits of individual people. Business-to-business market research explores product markets which are sold by one business to another. Travel writers can use their market research in a variety ways in order to gain a competitive edge, assuming that the information they gain is relevant, accurate, reliable, valid and current. Put simply, it allows a travel writer to forge ahead in business terms on the basis of sound, informed decisions – without relying on rumour, gut feeling or intuition. A six-step framework for market research (known as DECIDE) is the bedrock of many commercial entities, as follows:

D – Define the marketing problem
E – Enumerate the controllable and uncontrollable decision factors
C – Collect relevant information
I – Identify the best alternative
D – Develop and implement a marketing plan
E – Evaluate the decision and the decision process.

Basically, DECIDE advocates and facilitates a system that gathers accurate information to reflect a true state of affairs. It encourages questions to be asked about competitors, demand, market structure, regulations, economic trends, technological advances, and numerous other factors that make up the business environment. It also advocates an impartial measuring of results to determine the effectiveness of individual marketing activities. Market research and analysis should determine market segments, market targets, market forecasts and market positions – ultimately to determine how well a business is placed for success.

If this all sounds more suited to a large corporation than a travel writer – think again. A business is any entity created to provide goods or services to a consumer. That you are selling a talent or creative skill as a travel writer is immaterial when it comes to enhancing the success of its purpose. For example, market orientation is essentially basing a business's marketing plans around the marketing concept, and thus forging products to suit new consumer tastes. In simple terms, this is establishing what is in demand and evaluating if you are best placed to deliver it. All travel writers keen to maximise their income will be at a distinct disadvantage should they fail to ascertain this.

To apply the DECIDE model to travel writing, consider the following:

D – Determine what are your marketing weaknesses – are you doing all you can?
E – Evaluate what you can influence and what is out of your control
C – Collect all the information you need to give yourself a marketing push
I – Identify the marketing ideas that may work for you
D – Develop and implement a marketing plan
E – Evaluate what ideas are getting the best results – and why.

So, what next?

Everybody has some business acumen, even if they've not realised it. For example, we may be especially cute when it comes to shopping around for the best deals. Or we may be good at driving a hard bargain. As writers, we are adept at conveying something using mere words – a skill that is extremely effective when applied to written marketing and promotion tools. We are also practised researchers – using conventional sources (e.g. libraries or interviews) or digital sources (such as scouring the internet and using email Q&As).

Our work involves evaluation – be it in critique or story angles. By combining all these skills and utilising them in regards to our 'business' we are equipped to conduct a full marketing appraisal;

assessing demand (what magazines, newspapers and publishing are out there, what they need and how often) and how well placed we are to deliver it. For example, do we have the skills to meet the demand? Can we meet the need? What is the potential of the relationship in regards to volume and return? Part of every marketing strategy is the assessment of competition, so it is also important to keep an eye on the output of other travel writers in order to gauge what is 'selling well'.

❛ BRING YOUR CREATIVITY TO THE FORE

An Expert's View...

Lazy, boring writing is my biggest bugbear and I still see a lot from experienced writers, mostly due to over-commitment or rushing work.

Think about what you're writing and re-read what you've written.

Give advice but don't bore readers: a list of beaches or restaurants can sound the same – which one would you choose? What's on the menu? Can you hire sun loungers, buy drinks or should you bring your own? Mention the best part of a building, or what artwork to seek out.

Do you really need to describe everything as great, nice, lovely, tremendous, terrific, pretty, little, very, cute, etc. – what do they actually mean? Describe what you see, hear, smell and can touch. It brings a place to life. ❜

Fiona Quinn is a commissioning editor at Frommer's and began her travel writing career with a stint at one of the Grandes Ecoles in Paris. She spent eight years as editorial manager for Popout Maps both writing and researching guides such as Dubai, Paris, Venice, Los Angeles, New York, London and Bristol among many, many more. Fiona has also freelanced and updated guides for Thomas Cook including their HotSpots guide to Ibiza, with photos. (Visit: www.frommers.com/community/blogs/behind-the-guides.html)

Assessing your competitors

Ways to do this include the following.

♦ Staying up to date about how publishing outlets are doing. Are there new magazines on the market? Are some newspaper travel sections shifting their focus? Are new travel portals launching or doing better than others? Important developments include the appointment of new editors or publications that expand in regards to pagination. These types of developments can often bring about changes that offer opportunities for new writers.

♦ Conduct a warts-and-all evaluation of your working style. Are you organised, cost-efficient and well-informed? Do you know what's happening in the travel-writing world? Have you embraced technology or working modes that can heighten your efficiency? Do your potential clients know exactly what services you offer – or what makes you different? There may well be a thousand good reasons why you should be engaged as a travel writer – but if your potential clients are none the wiser your USPs (unique selling points) hold little value.

♦ Analyse your marketing strategy – what is its focus? What methods of promotion do you employ – and are they working? Ask yourself: what do my clients know about me in regards to skills (specialist areas and writing style); qualities (reliability and credibility); and delivery (capacity, availability and fees). Do they know how to reach you? Are they fully briefed about your travel history, upcoming trips and future projects? Consider a mix of conventional and digital initiatives to step up your marketing drives, from mail-shots, email bulletins and a website that includes photographs, a travel schedule, client references and a full set of contacts to Twitter entry or Facebook page – all excellent ways to appeal to a broad range of clients.

◆ Study your competition and the ebb and flow of the market. What is selling well (are there more articles about city breaks than cruises?). What's the demand like for your style, tone and specialist subject? Gauge what the real situation is in regards to commissions – your gut feeling may be way off beam, so it is important to take an honest look at the facts.

◆ Deliberate on how to improve all of the above. Build a list of marketing activities in direct response to the weak areas you've revealed. You should also use this opportunity to draw up a simple spreadsheet of accounts that outline your sales ledger (articles sold) and purchase ledger (expenses) month by month. Set against your overheads, this information will provide a clear indication of how you're faring in financial terms – a useful benchmark ahead of upping the ante in the marketing initiatives you introduce.

HOT TOOLS IN MARKETING

Like any other business, a travel writer should always keep an eye on how to be more creative and innovative in its marketing. Once a byword for pricey, glossy brochures, today's marketing efforts are increasingly low-cost social media marketing, such as Facebook. Love it or loathe it, Facebook is part of millions of people's daily routines over college age – so it is not only used by teenagers.

A large percentage of people log on each day in an office environment, including a growing number of corporate entities that use Facebook to keep up with current events and colleagues.

What is appealing about Facebook and Twitter is that they convey news before it ever hits the traditional media waves. Check out the umpteen online pages that offer advice on how to use Facebook to market your business – and you'll discover a surprising array of professional options, using Facebook Pages and Facebook Group. Twitter is also a hit with travel-related business and individuals (including writers). (Visit: www.facebook.com or www.twitter.com)

The following promotional tools form a central part of many successful travel writers marketing strategy:

◆ mailshots;
◆ email bulletins;
◆ websites;
◆ social networking sites;
◆ printed matter (business cards, letterheads, compliment slips and logo/corporate ID);
◆ promotional 'give-away' items.

The average editor or publisher is bombarded with hundreds of emails, dozens of instant messages, multiple urgent phone calls, a trilling mobile and several text messages a day – not to mention a mound of post and internal mail. Communication overload is a significant problem in the publishing world. Knowing how and when to make contact with an editor or publisher can be the difference between instigating a long-term, productive working relationship or being written off as an irritating nuisance.

Mailshots

Although the popularity of electronic bulletins has soared, conventional paper mailshots continue to play an important role in modern marketing. Many editors prefer to receive a pitch or introduction in both electronic and hard-copy format.

Mailshots are used by businesses of all sizes and can be an effective way of building customer relationships by post. Depending on the campaign, a mailshot can either be a 'warm' personalised letter to an identified contact or a 'cold' introduction.

Uscd well, postal marketing can be an extremely targeted, personal and creative way to engage potential clients to use your travel-writing services. Mailshots allow you to target new customers with either specific ideas or a general overview of how and where you work. Most business organisations open their post first thing in the morning when people are at their most receptive and decisive. Let's face it, when an inbox is overloaded, a pile of post can look a much more appealing prospect, especially to editors who favour tangible, personal, hard-copy communications.

According to Royal Mail, research shows that recipients may spend up to ten minutes reading mailshots. They digest the information in their own time and at their own pace, and then decide whether or not to act. Mail provides travel writers with a discrete, individualised environment to get a response from an individual customer. And there are many tools and techniques that can be used to help you get that response – but the golden rule is to ensure the mailshot is properly targeted. Writers should make the most of their talents to create engaging, persuasive mailshot content. It should be enticing, detailed and clearly outline what you have to say and sell. Of course, it is also imperative to provide the customer with the easiest way to respond – so be sure to include a good set of contact details, including email, phone number and website address.

Mailshots are also a simple way to stay in touch with existing customers. By targeting your message, and being personal, relevant, engaging and memorable, a postal marketing campaign can help your clients understand who you are, what you do and how your work could fit in with their plans. The Royal Mail puts the value of business secured via mailshot activities in the UK at £25 million – and there is absolutely no reason why a small slice of that couldn't be yours. In the last decade, despite changing and advancing technologies, mailshot expenditure has increased by a whopping 155%.

Consider the following.

◆ What are you trying to say?
◆ To whom?
◆ How are you going to say it in an impactful, engaging and compelling way?
◆ What is your pack going to look like or contain?
◆ What makes your product or service different?
◆ What would you like the recipient to remember above all else?
◆ What response are you asking for?

Mailshot propositions should be a balance between feature and benefit. Keep the message simple – it has to be understood clearly. Be sure to stress the benefits – you are selling the sizzle not the sausage. Mailshot marketing has the added benefit that it can be extremely specific, with regional and national client targeting, allowing you to target content accordingly to make it more personalised and relevant. Choose the paper, font and style of the mailshot to convey a professional image and be sure to check spelling and grammar – nothing will backfire more for a writer than a poorly composed letter littered with inky embarrassments.

Email bulletins

Many of the same rules apply to email targeting as they do to postal mailshots (see page 90). However, although they are often easier to execute, electronic campaigns require some additional planning and considerations. For example, spam filters like nothing more than to chew up emails from unrecognised senders – so it is important to give this issue some thought to ensure your bulletin reaches your intended target.

People want to know who a message is from, so emails are more effective if your email address conforms to a conventional, professional format. Paid-for email addresses carry great weight and appear more business-like regarding addresses that clearly state the name of the sender. For example, *David Harris < david@ example.com*, rather than *Guesswho@unknown.com*.

Use a clear, well thought out subject header that won't be picked up by the spam filter. Misspellings and abbreviations will also activate the spam filter. Apply the same principles for a cleverly crafted letter and ensure the tone and style is easy on the eye.

While many people think writing a subject or electronic message all in capital letters makes their messages stand out from the rest, nowadays the opposite may be true. Many people look at such a practice as amateurish, and doing this may decrease the level of respect the intended recipient has for you. Others may consider that using all capital letters is the same as shouting, and such a practice is considered rude. Worse, some over-aggressive spam filters may tag messages or message subjects containing all capital letters as junk, meaning your messages may never reach their destinations.

Never be tempted to send out an email to a large list of people – there is nothing more reviled than this impersonal approach and it is also poor etiquette. After all, we *all* want to feel as though we are worthy of an individually composed message, so by clearly issuing a mass communiqué you are likely to receive a lukewarm response.

Using a signature (a small block of text appended to the end of your messages) is a useful way of conveying your contact information. Many mailers can add a signature to their messages automatically. It identifies who you are and includes alternative means of contacting you (phone and fax are usual). In many systems, particularly where mail passes through gateways, your signature may be the only means by which the recipient can even tell who you are.

Try to break your message into logical paragraphs and restrict your sentences to sensible lengths. 'TXT-speak' '...f u wnt 2 use me I wld be gr8ful' – of any type – should never be used in professional email communication.

Electronic mail is all about communication with other people and, as such, some basic courtesy never goes amiss. However, don't assume that the simple fact that you have sent someone a message somehow obliges them to send a reply. Your copy – just like a postal mailshot – should be sufficiently compelling, enticing and engaging to encourage a response. Always read it before sending it and if possible, get others to check it too. Email is a highly personal medium and it is crucial to get the content, tone and balance spot-on.

Avoid attachments (as these can trigger spam filters and cause recipients anxiety about viruses). Include URLs to work examples or your website if at possible. If you only have scanned cuttings or PDF work samples, make their availability clear in the email. Post these onto your website if you can for ease of access.

Website

A website is one of the most inexpensive forms of marketing and, as a tool, it can serve many purposes. For travel writers, a website can often be a type of online CV outlining credentials, qualifications, awards and professional membership often with an archive of sample articles. Or it can be a more interactive online presence that combines the CV elements with maps of scheduled trips, blogs and chat rooms. Published travel writers and authors are also increasingly using the e-commerce gadgets to sell their books or link up to websites where their work is sold. Many travel writers run competitions, or ask visitors to their websites to post their comments, or vote in a weekly poll about a burning issue.

However, websites do not advertise themselves, so on their own they are unlikely to lead to work without publicity and promotion. To this end, it is important to include your website address on flyers, business cards, directories and mailshots. Used in conjunction with other marketing tools, a website can offer numerous additional features not available from the conventional advertising route.

When developing ideas for your website, consider the following.

◆ What is the purpose of your website?

◆ What is your intended target audience?

◆ Are you targeting your niche skills or general services?

◆ What do you need in terms of content?

◆ What keywords will you need (consider your domain name, meta-tags, title, subject lines, page header and each page you write)?

◆ Are you going to use pay-per-click ads to drive traffic directly to your site?

◆ Do you need an e-commerce facility to sell your work online?

◆ Are there links you can maximise (from associations, publishers and colleagues) that could help drive traffic to your site?

Some of the most effective websites are simple in design – to get ideas it pays to conduct some research by simply surfing the net for formats that catch your eye. Information should be neatly laid out, with pages that download quickly and are logically organised. Websites should be easy to navigate and informative and, while 'bells and whistles' features may appeal, it is important to distinguish between the gimmicky gadgets that offer very little and the gizmo that adds extra benefits.

Before considering what style of website you need, it is crucial to identify what it is that you need it to do. A basic website will allow you to start small and add more features as the need arises – as long as you've bought a website package that allows for this organic growth. DIY websites have improved dramatically over the past decade – and offer a wide range of inexpensive template options (from £100) that can be easily customised.

However, you may prefer to ask an expert to create one for you. This will be considerably pricier but a professional website designer may be able to suggest functionality that you didn't know existed. You may be able to sell your entire portfolio of photographs, post news and fresh developments and engage with potential clients and fellow-travellers all over the world. It's a way for your customer base to find you, to know how to get in touch with you. Many prospective clients may prefer to deal with a person they feel they 'know' – and a website presence is a great way to achieve this. With a biography page, a section on past or upcoming trips and some photographs that depict you in different locations – you are more human and more tangible than an email address.

Your website may also be able to earn you income from click-through links to commercial portals. It can also facilitate reciprocal marketing deals. If you are working with publishers in non-English-speaking countries then it may be important to consider language options. Joining writers' networks and professional membership organisations will also provide an opportunity to enjoy the benefits of links to other websites.

Keen to be a searchable website that ranks high in MSN or Google results? Then consider following search engine optimisation (SEO) tips. Though time-consuming, improving SEO is a worthwhile project. A simple internet search under 'SEO tips' will reveal a wealth of pointers as to how to register your website to benefit from improved search results.

Social networking sites

One of the commonest reasons stated by small businesses for not embracing social networking is that they can't measure results. Many are so intimidated by the 'technology' side of social networking that they haven't made the connection to how simple a networking model really is.

In 2008, over $40 billion was spent on social networking in the US alone by businesses who understood the marketing potential. Social marketing online allows people to connect with each other in a virtual gathering through networking which has been a core tactic for marketing long before the internet came of age. The explosion of services such as LinkedIn, Twitter, Facebook and Ning has made this version of the electronic exchange easier to manage without leaving the office.

Many people use multiple social networks as well as You Tube and Flickr – and all are used by travel writers, authors, publishers, editors and journalists. The audience for LinkedIn more than doubled in 2007–2008, while Facebook and Twitter have become de facto business networks – with social networking expenditure expected to reach an estimated $210 million by 2012.

Printed matter

Despite the trend for online or electronic marketing tools, there is still a place for conventional printed matter, such as business cards, letterheads, leaflets, brochures and compliment slips. Even if you rarely print and post a letter, you will almost certainly need to create a logo as part of developing a corporate ID for use online.

A corporate ID is something eye-catching, unique and visual that immediately tells a potential or existing client that something relates to you. It may not be as grand as a massive logo but may be a font or style of design that triggers recognition with the client. Think of any business, big or small, and almost all will have a corporate ID. Just like individuals, businesses have their own distinct identities and a logo, colours and style can help convey a message of who and what they are – and what they stand for.

Creating a new logo is always a challenge and is something that requires some thought. As it will stay with you throughout the life of your business and represent you to clients, it is your window to the world, defining you and presenting your values in every communication. Therefore a design should be professional and timeless so that it offers longevity without ageing. A simple idea is best as it conveys a single – and therefore strong – streamlined message that lodges in people's minds.

A logo is usually central to the corporate identity of a business. Corporate IDs act as a signal for the type of business that you are through symbolism and shape. It should be an idea that pulls together why you do what you do, what it is you are actually going to do and how you are going to do it. Although big-business spends millions on creating just the right corporate ID it is more than possible to effect the same on a shoestring budget. For a limited outlay, you can signal that you are polished, professional and focused with a business-minded approach to your field.

Scribble down some ideas that represent your business philosophy, ethics, goals and achievements to see what transpires. Get a graphic designer to turn these ideas into something that meets your brief. This design can then be used across all of your marketing initiatives in printed matter, websites and electronic campaigns. Many start-up businesses put off designing a logo and marketing materials 'until they get a few clients'. However, getting those initial clients can be significantly easier with a well-thought-out corporate ID to help give a marketing drive extra push.

Promotional 'give-aways'

As a stand-alone tool, promotional gizmos are unlikely to win you new clients. Yet, the subtle power of promotional products shouldn't be underestimated. Give-away promotional items can help to reinforce other important marketing activities. They won't make the phone ring off the hook, but they can help raise your profile and make potential clients aware that you exist. Sometimes a promotional keychain can succeed where emails and calls don't.

Promotional products play a distinctive role in getting a message to the client in a different way to the norm. Choose the right item and it could well become a living advertisement for you and what you do. However, given that results are difficult to measure, promotional give-aways are often ignored by small businesses with tight budgets. Because of this, travel writers will soon discover that their potential clients are rarely targeted in this way. Consequently, a well-thought-out promotional item will have greater impact on the basis that it is a novelty. However, it is important to consider the link between the gizmo, the message and the recipient in order for this type of campaign to work.

Many suppliers have vast catalogues of thousands of give-away options ready for printing with your contacts and logo. However, the quality varies dramatically, so always ask for a sample before you commit to an order. Choose from a range of mugs, pens, pencils and stress balls. A growing number of companies are stocking items on a travel or writing theme. Consider the following ideas:

◆ coasters with luggage-tag design;
◆ mouse-mats with world map designs;
◆ globe-topped keychains;
◆ book marks with a 'passport-style' stamp;
◆ sticky notes in the style of a travel checklist.

You can also get travel toothbrush kits, travel alarm clocks, luggage belts, travel wallets, travel sewing kits, adaptors and luggage weighing scales printed with your name and logo. Items start at about 70p each with minimum orders of around 200 units. However, this sector is extremely competitive, so don't be afraid to haggle for a deal.

CLIENT RELATIONSHIPS

According to umpteen surveys, a service-driven business is able to charge up to 9% more for the goods and service it offers simply because it is client-focused. Good, proactive businesses also grow twice as fast as the average set-up. These are powerful incentives for travel writers to apply some first-rate customer service skills to their marketing mode.

Today, more than ever, good customer care matters because keeping existing customers is easier than finding new ones. Each and every client should be viewed as part of your sales force. A satisfied customer is not only more likely to give you more work but can also become an extremely efficient promotional tool. Recommendations are important in any business sector – and the travel writing field is no different. Delivering good customer service is also highly rewarding and satisfying. It is also good for self-esteem as there is nothing nicer than knowing that you've done a job well and made a good impression. Put simply, maximising travel-writing potential isn't just about what's written on the page.

Equally, poor service has a cost penalty. It costs up to five times as much to go out and get a new customer as to retain those we have. A customer who is happy with every aspect of the way in which you work is more likely to offer repeat commissions. The goal of every travel writer keen to maximise income is to nurture excellent customer relationship to secure on-going business. Research suggests that customers who encounter poor service tell at least nine other people about it. To become established as a writer with an untarnished reputation, your goal should be excellence in every aspect.

It is a standard human reaction to respond to the way we are treated by others. We tend to act according to the behaviours we encounter and the style of interaction we experience. If a client is being uncooperative, uncommunicative or off-hand it is easy to put this down to stress or a personality trait. However, these problem areas could well be a direct result of a flawed customer service relationship. Ask yourself the following questions.

◆ Am I getting the customer reactions that I deserve?

◆ Are the styles of communications hitting the mark?

◆ Could I relate to my customer better?

◆ How can I improve the situation?

Customer service is one area where a savvy, business-minded travel-writing professional can shine. By placing great importance on cultivating intense loyalty among regular customers, a good freelancer can maximise the benefits that strong relationships bring. Service is a major differentiator – it can separate one travel writer from another. Even though most businesses understand the principles of customer care, only 6% actually apply them effectively. Successfully placing customer satisfaction at the core of your business can go a long way to ensuring you have the edge over your competition.

Deliver high standards of customer service

Delivering high standards of customer service means going that 'extra mile' to deliver an order (commission) with added value (exceeding the brief) using the standard business principles of pre-sales, delivery and after-care.

Another key way to differentiate is to focus more on listening than on talking. Many writers are so keen to sell their services they do too much talking. To meet or exceed customer needs it pays to really listen because this allows you to get beyond the simple sales exchange to better understand their unstated needs. Once you do that, not only will you have a better connection, you'll be able to exceed their expectations.

When people feel listened to, they feel valued and respected. Studies suggest that over 65% of customers switch suppliers because of a perceived attitude of indifference. So, once you have the order, it is important to show that it matters, because if you deliver it with indifference and zero after-sales customer care, the interaction may fail to leave a positive impression – even if the writing hits the mark.

Not sure how your customer service skills match up? Then put yourself in the shoes of the client and consider how you prefer to be treated. Use the following checklist to manage your customer-focused approach.

* Do you make your customers feel welcomed, respected and valued?

* Do you understand their needs and place them at the heart of your business practice?

* Do you manage customer care issues in a consistent and confident manner – and view customer complaints as valuable feedback? Are you calm when dealing with difficult issues?

* Do you provide services at a time and place that suits your customers? Do your customers know who you are and what your core business values are?

* Are you available? This is an important point for travel writers to ponder. Can your customers contact you when they need to? Do you respond in a reliable, timely way?

* Do you take pride in your work? If so, is this communicated to the customer in actions as well as words?

- Do you honour promises? Do you communicate problems or delays?

- Do you avoid post-sales follow up? Or do you view this as part of the service? Shying away from after-sales communiqués can demonstrate a lack of confidence in your product, sending a negative message to clients. It also lessens the chances of being able to ask for extra work (see Asking for More on page 109) and will hinder your efforts in developing good, productive long-term working relationships.

Having identified the principles of customer care it is important to put them into practice. Empty pledges will almost certainly backfire so it is paramount to incorporate them into how you work – they are meaningless as undelivered promises.

This sign on a customer service training company's wall really says it all!
Some business enterprises make things happen; some business enterprises watch what happens, and some business enterprises wonder what happened.

Top tips for delivering customer excellence

- Think of customers as individuals (one size definitely doesn't fit all).

- Know who your customers are (understand whom you are dealing with).

- Ensure your customers know who you are.

- Understand and anticipate their needs.

- Go the extra mile to exceed expectations (do more than meet the brief).

- Listen to what your customers say (don't over-talk to make the sale).

- Ask for feedback and invite comments and suggestions.

- Differentiate your business to make it 'visible'.

- Deal with difficult issues, don't avoid them.

- Be reliable, consistent and dependable (you'll be easier to trust).

- Make your customers feel valued.

- Be approachable (and easily contactable).

- Thank them for allowing you to pitch, even if they don't commission.

- View every interaction as important (not just those that lead to work).

At some point or other, it is inevitable that you'll need to deal with the occasional disgruntled editor or customer – no matter how wonderful your writing is. You may have been committed to meeting the brief and slogged away for hours to craft a piece to exceed your client's expectations. You may have filed your article, content in the knowledge that you went that extra mile.

However dedicated you are as a writer and despite all your carefully implemented customer service standards, you may still get the call that indicates something has gone awry. Problems can occur despite all your efforts for a smooth, client-focused interaction. However, by applying some basic customer service principles a tricky situation can be diffused leaving a client relationship intact. You can not only save the sale but also possibly create more business by simply facing up to the fact that, somewhere down the line, a problem has occurred.

Although it is hard to hear that a customer isn't happy, it is important to remember that it is not a personal attack. Let them talk as long as they need to, not only to get it off their chest, but to thoroughly explain the problem. Never cut in. Listen carefully to fully understand the scope of the issue – if you don't, you'll be highly unlikely to be able to put it right. Taking the time to listen will send out a positive message that you are interested in solving the problem. Once the initial niggle has been vented, you'll be able to ask questions regarding the situation that will lead to resolving it in a positive manner.

Once you understand why the customer is upset, apologise – even if you don't agree with their complaint. By accepting the situation and taking ownership of it the customer will feel valued. It will also signal that you are keen to work towards a resolution. Remove emotion from the problem and empathise with the customer. It may be clear what can bring the situation to a satisfactory conclusion, for example, rewriting a paragraph or adding a sidebar. Other problems may require further discussion to accommodate the unspecific needs of the customer, for example when an article 'just isn't what I was looking for'. Show a clear commitment to resolving their problem – and whatever promises you make to the customer, be sure to follow up.

Getting customer feedback

In many instances, customer feedback is an opportunity for change. If a complaint is valid regarding customer service, then keep improving those areas over which you have control. For example, if the root of the problem is a miscommunication then address this issue.

If an editor has highlighted weak areas in your writing style, then consider ways to improve this aspect. Draw parallels with your own customer service experience, for example when you make a valid complaint regarding a mobile phone that doesn't suit your needs. If the shop concerned makes every effort to resolve the situation to your ultimate satisfaction, it is likely to reinforce your impression of the company in a positive way. Indeed, it will probably encourage you to buy from them again. However, should they fail to accept the issue, duck out of accepting responsibility and offer little in the way of resolution, it will signal the termination of your relationship – and the likelihood of any future sales. Worse, you'll almost certainly moan about your gripe to anyone who'll listen.

Retaining your customers

Having considered what's paramount in winning and retaining customers it is important to acknowledge how easy it is to lose them. Customer retention and satisfaction drive profits and make for a more rewarding career. It is far less expensive to cultivate an existing customer base and sell more services to them than it is to seek new, single-transaction customers. Strange as it may seem, many people in business actively work in a way that will almost certainly lose them customers. Consider the following to ascertain whether you are guilty of driving customers away.

- Does getting rid of an annoying customer give you more satisfaction than keeping one?

- Do you attempt to get away with extra billing without discussing it first?

- Do you tell half-truths to your customers or intentionally mislead them?

- Do you renege on promises and fail to deliver your commitments?

- Are you impossible to contact? Do you sometimes fail to return calls?

- Do you disrespect the credentials of a customer or deal with them in a condescending manner?

- Do you blame problems on others and avoid personal responsibility?

- Do you value quantity over quality? How good is your quality control?

- Do you remind your customer that you are the only option?

- Do you continually reinforce how important you are to them?

- Do you make them feel less important than other 'priority' customers?

- Are you indignant when they criticise or offer feedback?

- Do you never say 'thank you' for fear of appearing to need them?

A sure way to lose customers in travel writing is get the balance wrong when it comes to building up a profitable business. It is important to develop sales to ensure you are maximising your income potential, but this should never impact on the quality you deliver. Quality control is directly related to customer service. Dissatisfaction is almost always a result of sloppy workmanship when a writer has failed to apply the usual checks to ensure the work is up to scratch. Mistakes can also happen when a writer tries to deviate from the norm or fails to allow sufficient time to craft a piece that exceeds the brief. When quality suffers, the whole foundation of the client–supply relationship is rocked.

Most businesses, such as manufacturing, have checks in place to ensure that a product isn't released until it meets a consistent level of quality. Travel writers need to maintain similar quality control checks, especially during particularly busy periods. Your client will expect this delivery to meet their expectations, regardless of whatever else you're juggling work-wise at the same time. They aren't remotely interested in your other deadlines or commitments – so it is important to take every step not to disappoint them. Once their perception of you has altered it is extremely hard to revert however understanding they may seem.

Ask yourself: is this what my client is expecting? Also check that it meets your usual standards as a stand-alone piece of work. Check the following.

- Composition and content (does it mirror the brief and say what you want it to say?).

- Structure (does it build well? Are the paragraphs in the right order? Are you repeating yourself at any point?).

◆ Organisation (is this clear and logical? Does the subject flow with the use of paragraphs for each directional shift?).

◆ Spelling (including variations if writing for overseas publications using Americanised English). Don't rely solely on a spell-check function, scrutinise the pages with a keen eye.

◆ Sentences and punctuation (at sentence level is the content ordered correctly? This is especially important to reassess if you cut and pasted text to reorganise the structure. Check that sentences convey the message, replacing repetitive use of words).

Cut it back if it is over the word count and check that it has been written in the specific style the editor or publisher has requested (for example, double-spaced in Times New Roman 12 point with italicised foreign words and bold headlines). Add a header and footer that clearly states your name, email address and telephone number (as this saves your editor from having to root around for your contacts should they need to discuss the piece with you). If you know the issue number and title then add this too.

Check what format the client has asked the work to be submitted in. Most ask for it to emailed to them, sometimes with a hard-copy version sent by post. However, this could be in varying format, for example a normal MS Word document or an RTF file. If the deadline is 12 noon on 1 August, then be sure to deliver the work before the specified time. Some editors provide specific instructions for uploading work to file servers or request that work is emailed to a colleague. Never assume that everyone works in the same way.

Asking for more
Part of marketing a business is utilising winning pitches as a base

on which to build. It can sometimes take months of nurturing a blossoming relationship with a potential client to gain a commission. Of course you're delighted – you've won a job through persistence, persuasion and continued effort. However, it is important to remember that you did not work so hard on this client to win only one piece of work. A single commission will not pay the mortgage. It is also not an on-going client relationship but a base on which to build further business.

If you've produced a good piece of travel writing to an exacting brief, it will give you the perfect opportunity to ask for more work. You may want to couch the request for work during a feedback discussion. Or you may prefer to pitch again as you did before. Organise your questions well and emphasise how much you enjoyed the project. A marked degree of enthusiasm and hunger for the work will help – not all of your well-established competitors will feel the need to do this. Ask your client about upcoming feature schedules and demonstrate that you can offer them something of value. Phrase your request for work in terms of providing further help and support, such as: 'What have you got on the horizon that I may be able to help you with?'. In other words, demonstrate a level of willingness, enthusiasm and genuine concern for their work that takes you ahead of the other writers. Overall, you have earned the right to ask for more work once you have earned the client's respect. So, be sure so seize the opportunity to ask for more in a style you feel comfortable with – but never be afraid to ask.

Meeting the editor

Believe it or not, very few magazine editors and commissioning editors at book publishers ever get to meet the writers or authors they engage. So much of the commissioning and subsequent editing work is done by email and telephone these days. So it not uncommon for working relationships to span many years without any personal, face-to-face contact.

Travel writers prepared to invest the time and the budget will find that issuing invitations to meet over coffee or lunch can be highly productive. Of course, few editors and publishers have unlimited time to devote to such practices but most should be able to spare an hour to 'put a face to a name'. Ask them to suggest a venue (it'll save you from having to make a choice) – most will opt for the nicest place within walking distance of their office. Meeting in this way allows the editor or publisher to take time out from their busy schedule – yet provides the legitimate excuse of being work-related. At the same time, it provides the writer with the ideal opportunity to form a bond, convey a good impression and subtly explore the possibilities of work.

With the long, boozy lunches of the 1980s ancient history, most publishers and editors will only be able to spare an hour or so. Make the most of this 60 minutes as it may be hard to secure another meeting. Encourage them to talk freely about their work and the projects that are upcoming or on-going. Maximise the opportunity to make it very clear that you want to work with them in the future. Be professional, comfortable and quietly assured but never use a lunch for a full-blown hard sell. Arrive well prepared with cuttings and business cards and view the occasion as a relationship-forging event, unless your lunch partner openly invites you to sell yourself and your ideas.

❛WINE, WOMEN AND WRITERS

An Expert's View...

We launched Women in Travel (WiT) in 2007 as an informal networking forum for women who work in the travel industry. We hold the events in a central London venue on a quarterly basis and invite representatives of domestic and international tourist boards, tour operators, airlines, other travel organisations and the media.

It's all done on a very relaxed basis – we ask guests not to bring along brochures, as we prefer everyone to network and have a good time, rather than going in for the heavy sell. I think the reason WiT has been so successful is because it's so informal and there has been such strong industry support. High-profile regulars include the founder and editor-in-chief of Wanderlust, *Lyn Hughes, and Lupita Gayala, deputy director of the Mexico Tourism Board, as well as tour operators like Kuoni, TUI and Abercrombie & Kent.*

There's a lot of 'what do you do, how many pets have you got' kind of talk, but there's also a fair bit of chatting about everyday life. After a few glasses of wine there's always a few people updating us on the latest trials and tribulations of their love life – usually to complete strangers! We usually hold a prize draw for gifts donated by attendees, such as cookery books and hotel stays, which go down really well, although we no longer need to incentivise people to attend, as word has got around that it's an event worth attending. And there's nothing more rewarding than receiving an email from someone in the travel business saying that they've heard of Women in Travel and could they come along to the next event. The answer is invariably yes – the more the merrier. ❜

Susie Tempest is a board director at The Saltmarsh Partnership (www.saltmarshpr.co.uk) and a founder member of Women in Travel (WiT).

Consumer travel fairs and travel trade events also often provide an opportunity to mingle with commissioning editors. However, it is important to gauge the etiquette at each networking soirée. Some are social with some subtle opportunities to 'connect' with the right people but are not vehicles for actively seeking commissions. Others are business gatherings where networking is the prime purpose. The travel industry has also spawned a variety of social networks, such as Women in Travel (WiT). Many creative writing courses include talks by guest speakers, many of whom are commissioning editors and publishers. Membership organisations, such as the British Guild of Travel Writers (BGTW) also stage numerous well-subscribed events at which writers, publishers and magazine editors can exchange ideas (see page 253).

❝NEVER BE AFRAID TO ASK

An Expert's View...

I was working with a major travel book publisher for the first time, contributing to an anthology of travel tales and anecdotes. Having delivered my copy early I then talked the editor through the piece and was thrilled to hear that she was delighted with what I'd written. "It's absolutely perfect!" she trilled and asked me if she could use it as an example of the style and standard of work she wanted. Of course I agreed, but sensing there was another project on the horizon, I enquired if I might be able to help out with anything upcoming. "Of course!" she said, sounding relieved. "I didn't want to ask you – as I know you're so busy. Actually, I was about to commission it all this afternoon to other writers – so I'm so glad you brought it up."

This taught me a lesson in asking for work and to never assume that I'd be in the running for projects, simply on the basis that I'd delivered on previous jobs. You've nothing to lose from asking – and it can often make a commissioning editor's life considerably easier by proactively throwing your hat into the ring. **,**

Sarah Woods (www.sarahwoods.co.uk)

Working with others/referrals

As you develop a network of writing contacts and meet more fellow travel writers, the chances are you will meet individuals with whom you feel you could pair up work-wise. These may be people who are like-minded, or have similar writing or working styles, or with whom you have travel experiences in common.

In order to maximise revenue-generating potential, it is important to explore the possibilities these potential partnerships could bring. For example, it may be that together you are able to win larger pitches or take on labour-intensive projects. Combining your skills with other talents and strengths can often be an astute way to approach work on travel supplements and large-scale travel and tourism reports.

Another way to benefit from a growing circle of travel-writing industry colleagues is to develop referrals. So many people are reluctant to ask for referrals from their fellows, yet these are often worth their weight in gold, as there is no greater basis on which to win a pitch than having been recommended by a trusted source. Many people believe that there is no need to ask for them since their work speaks volumes. If this were true than I wonder how much *more* business they could be doing if they were more proactive in asking for referrals. A cornerstone principle of any marketing/lead generation programme is getting into the habit and comfort of seeking new leads – and a referral is the best lead of all.

You may like to create a 'thank you scheme' to recognise the generosity of those who have passed work your way – around 10–15% of the fee is standard. Once the commission is confirmed, calculate your budget and spend it on a gift-wrapped bottle of wine with a hand-written note of gratitude. You'll be surprised how much additional work this simple act can generate. Of course, a particularly content client can be an excellent ambassador for your work, so it is worth asking for a testimonial for your website, a reference or a direct referral. Most editors and publishers are more than happy to vouch for you as long as it is to a non-competing publication. After all, it reinforces their commissioning credentials and ability to recruit good travel-writing talent.

Memberships
According to a piece in *The Times* (January 2009), there are clear economic benefits of professional membership. This is estimated at around £81,000 for a person holding a professional qualification and at £71,000 for a member of a professional institute – no small amount. A 9% increase in the probability of being employed is another perk of being a member of a professional body.

What is a professional membership?
A professional membership is basically a subscription to a professional organisation – and, like any other sector, travel

writing has a number of membership options. Most aren't travel-specific, spanning journalism and author societies, with the British Guild of Travel Writers the largest and best-established professional member organisation.

Professional organisations offer members activities and services that place a framework around quality standards, professional development and maintaining currency within their specific field. Benefits vary from one organisation to another but typically include the following.

- ◆ **Credibility** Professional organisations set minimum quality standards for membership; therefore communicating that you have a professional membership also indicates that you are accredited. Being part of such an organisation should set you apart from others in standards, credibility and values.

- ◆ **Networking** Most organisations arrange regular events and activities that allow networking among professional colleagues. These can range from formal dinners to social events and offer an opportunity for people to expand and share knowledge, learn from others and gain career-based information and awareness.

- ◆ **Communications** Regular newsletters and bulletins provide members with access to information communicated either in printed form, journals or on the organisation's website.

- ◆ **Forums** Participating in a two-way discussion or sharing your views on blogs with experienced people about professional issues allows members to have their own thoughts heard and clarified.

- **Discounts** These may also be given by associated organisations for joint memberships or affiliation.

- **Professional development** Access to specific events and training that provide opportunities for learning that is specific to your profession and helps keep your skills current.

- **Services** Membership can also lead to discounted services on insurances, goods, services and transport.

Memberships add value to a CV as they show that you have sought out and subscribed to an organisation as an indication of your level of involvement as a professional. However, membership should not be passive but an active participation. Regular networking events allow colleagues to meet, interact and present themselves professionally and positively to people who may potentially be able to offer work. Membership offers an opportunity to contribute to forums, and present and discuss your own ideas, thoughts and findings. You may also eventually be able to take a position within the organisation, maybe initially on a working party and later, with experience, on the board.

❝ WHY JOIN THE BRITISH GUILD OF TRAVEL WRITERS?

An Expert's View...

As a long-term member (and current Chair) of the Guild I have experienced and witnessed the benefits that belonging to the organisation brings. On a personal level, since I joined about 20 years ago, it has always paid for itself many times over in commissions from other members (including the joining fee).

However, the networking opportunities are not linked solely to meetings – we have an excellent website with a lively discussion forum, a monthly newsletter, a quarterly newsletter that goes out to the industry, a live RSS feed and the Yearbook.

The Guild gets your biographical details onto the desk of every major commissioning editor and travel PR in the UK and an increasing number overseas as well, plus offering website space for you to create a portfolio of your work as a showcase instead of, or linked to, your own website. We also offer options to display your work on our home page.

As the Guild profile rises, several PRs and editors have said to me that they go straight to the Guild members as an easy, reliable place to find good contributors.

As with everything, you get out of Guild membership what you are prepared to put in. I have invested a great deal and reaped huge rewards including plenty of help, advice and support from other members (from dealing with the downturn in guidebook publishing, to how to tackle a new career as a blogger). Socially, I have made some really good friends and lots of superb contacts. I have also learned a huge amount (we are also now running professional training days) and had a lot of fun. ❜

Melissa Shales is an award-winning travel writer and author and chair of the British Guild of Travel Writers. Go to: www.bgtw.org to visit the Membership section for details on the benefits of membership and how to apply.

4

Building a Brand

> *If you reject the food, ignore the customs, fear the religion and avoid the people, you might better stay home.*

James Michener

When building a brand, the name and logo are the least important things. It is the product, the service and the standards of the business that enables a brand to grow. You need to know who your customer is and who your customer is not. Branding is who you are and what you stand for.

Every business strives to create a brand identity because to build a brand can lead to brand loyalty. This is when a customer buys into the philosophy and trading style of a supplier – and subscribes to all, or most, of what it represents. To build a brand, you need to know what it is you want to communicate to your clients – and how. For example, if you want them to think you are innovative, dependable and reliable, then this is the message you should convey – but only once you've identified that this is what they actually need.

Generally speaking, there is an accepted sequence to developing a brand, just as there is to developing the business itself. Many of the steps which suit big business may help travel writers to crystallise their ideas about the following three points because they will bring a greater focus to who they are and what they do.

◆ writing a vision statement;

◆ crafting a mission statement;

◆ identifying their unique selling points (USPs).

A well-crafted mission and vision statement can be the glue that binds your purpose and dreams together. It provides you with a benchmark on which to grow your travel-writing business, by defining where you are and what you do – and where you want to be.

WRITING YOUR VISION STATEMENT

Although it is easy to write off a vision statement as a conjured-up corporate puff, it can be particularly useful for a small business keen to define its goals and focus. Create it during the start-up phase to give you inspiration. It will also provide a framework for all your strategic planning as it answers a travel writer's question, 'What do I want my work to lead to?' Basically, you're articulating your dreams and hopes for your business. Doing this at the start provides you with a constant point of reference and a reminder of what you are trying to build.

> **Example: a vision statement for a budding travel author.**
> Within the next five years, John Smith will be a recognised name within the travel guide market with multiple titles published in Latin America. By 2015, he will have increased his revenue from travel writing to £50,000 per annum by becoming internationally known as an expert in Latin American tourism, travel and indigenous cultures.

CRAFTING YOUR MISSION STATEMENT

Mission statements aren't just for vast enterprises but work just as well for small businesses, because they define a company's fundamental purpose. For a travel writer, a mission statement answers the question, 'Why do I do what I do?'.

Take time to craft your mission statement as it articulates your company's purpose – both as it relates to you and to your potential client base. However, other than that, there is no standard style when it comes to the format of a mission statement. They are as varied as the businesses they describe.

As a travel writer or author, use your mission statement to broadly define your present capabilities, customer focus, activities, and business makeup – unlike the vision statement (see above), a mission statement reflects where you are *now*, not where you want to be in the future. It serves as a baseline for effective business planning.

> **Example: John Smith is a forward-thinking travel writer.**
> John Smith continuously strives to exceed the needs of his customers. He offers a unique package of travel experience, writing talent, credentials and skills and is a dedicated, ideas-driven professional.

The following are telltale signs that a brand is weak.

- **You can't describe in one sentence what differentiates your brand from your competitors.** Can you sum up what you can do that competitors can't? If you can't, you need to work on establishing your brand identity.

- **You can't sum up your mission, vision and values in one sentence.** Enough said.

- **No one can remember your logo.** You may have spent ages crafting a design that incorporated elements of your personality – but if it isn't memorable, recognisable and likeable it won't work. Keep it simple and use something that is yours.

- **Your clients wouldn't notice if you disappeared.** Yes, this one is hard to swallow, but it is important to consider. If you vanished off the radar, would they wonder where you are? If not, you have a profile problem.

- **People still liken you to others.** Sure, it is good to be associated with other travel writers, but it is preferable to be recognised as a talent in your own right. If you are indistinguishable from other writers, you haven't built a strong enough brand.

IDENTIFYING YOUR UNIQUE SELLING POINTS

For years, USP has been a buzzword favoured by business trainers across the globe. Marketing seminars often devote full days to stressing the importance of 'USPs' (unique selling points or unique selling propositions). Donald Trump has built his entire empire on maximising his USP potential. Yet the simple principle of identifying what makes your business unique can apply as easily to an individual as to a multi-billion-dollar corporation.

Don't expect a potential client to immediately understand why they should commission you – it's a better strategy to state the benefits you provide rather than leave it to an editor or publisher to work it out for themselves. Your USP is the unique thing you can offer that your competitors can't. It's your 'competitive edge' – the reason you are different from all the other writers out there. USPs should highlight why customers should buy from you and you alone. Individually, each USP should indicate an area of strength or uniqueness. Combined, they should make you stand out from the crowd and ensure you get the recognition – and the commissions – you deserve.

What makes you different from all the millions of other writers pitching and penning all over the world? This is the question to ask ahead of compiling a list of USPs. Clear your mind and your desk and scribble down exactly what it is that differentiates you from the throng. Write down everything, you can always fine-tune the list later. It may help to box ideas into headings, such as Experience; Quality; Style; Credentials. Or it could be that a more free-flowing brainstorming approach will deliver better results. What you produce can be used in a variety of ways, from a biography to a profile. It should form the basis of all your core marketing activities and will, in time, help to reinforce your business as you build and develop it further.

Defining your USPs provides an opportunity for you to present yourself in the best possible light. Potential clients are looking for skills that shine out. They want writers with energy and enthusiasm. It may be an alien concept to blow your own trumpet in this way but in marketing terms, USPs are all about 'you'. For example, millions of businesses promote themselves as offering 'quality, professional, friendly service' – but this fails to differentiate what they do from anyone else claiming exactly the same. Using a message that doesn't sound like everyone else's is the only way to succeed when promoting your USPs.

❛ IT PAYS TO BE DIFFERENT

An Expert's View...

Simply telling a commissioning editor you're off on a trip, or need a commission to go on a trip, is not a pitch. It's called trying to get a freebie without thinking of what editors really need for their magazine. The best pitches are those that fit the publication's readership, content and history. ABTA Golf *is an annual publication, so pitching exactly the same feature as one that ran the year before is plain lazy. Editors want fresh angles – granted writers cannot reinvent the wheel every time, but they can pour fresh water into the bucket such as newsworthy features, off-the-wall ideas and lateral thinking. Just read the previous editions and put together a pitch that follows a simple but efficient structure: why you should run a feature about x; what's so exciting about it; how my treatment is going to be different from what you might have read/run before; and by the way I am going there soon/I was there recently, so will have the freshest material possible. That should do the trick.* ❜

Sonia Soltani works as Project Editor at Absolute Publishing Ltd where she's responsible for the *ASTA Worldwide Destination Guide 2009/10, ABTA Golf 2010* and the *ABTA Members' Handbook 2010.* She also contributes to APL's other titles including *ABTA Magazine, Welcome2London, Escape* and *Spa Secrets.* Sonia has a Postgraduate Diploma in Magazine Journalism from City University and worked on a range of trade titles including *Property Week, Building Design* and *Building,* before joining *Travel Trade Gazette* (TTG) as Deputy Supplements Editor in January 2007.
(Visit: www.absolutepublishing.com)

Once you've made a list of every feature that you can offer a potential client, write beside it an explanation of what it can mean in business terms. By doing this, a simple page of skills and experience is converted into a sales benefit. Do the same exercise for your competitors too – any features that stand out as being superior to your competition are strong USPs. Don't rush this simple exercise; allow your brainstorming to produce a flow of ideas that organically feed off each other. You will soon start to see the main benefits for customers to use you and your services – and what makes you unique. When you identify your USP, make sure it's something that really matters to potential customers. There's no point in being the best in the industry for something that nobody cares about.

TOP TIPS FOR IDENTIFYING YOUR USPs

♦ First, make notes about what you can offer of value to a publisher or editor – move beyond the basics common to all other writers and examine what it is about your service that is unique. If you can, involve other people in the exercise in order to appreciate an outside perspective. Incorporate the feedback you've received from clients, colleagues, tutors and fellow writers.

♦ Now identify your major competitors, being sure to be as objective as you can. Identify different competitors' strengths and weaknesses. From this, develop a simple, easily communicated statement of your USP.

♦ Once you've created a profile of what makes you stand out from the millions of writers on Planet Earth, make sure the USPs are of value to the publishing world. If they don't matter, they are worthless. Scrutinise your USPs to ensure they reflect what makes your business different. They should be a driving force in persuading customers to come to you, not the competition.

For example, approach your attributes by asking the following questions.

- Qualifications, experience and credentials – what makes you unique?
- Characteristics, style and approach – what makes you unique?
- Location, mobility, access and contacts – what makes you unique?
- Recommendations, testimonials and references – what makes you unique?

Then repeat the exercise with the following shift in emphasis.

- Qualifications, experience and credentials – what do my clients value?
- Characteristics, style and approach – what do my clients value?
- Location, mobility, access and contacts – what do my clients value?
- Recommendations, testimonials and references – what do my clients value?

Then repeat the exercise with the focus on your major competitors.

- Qualifications, experience and credentials – what makes them unique?
- Characteristics, style and approach – what makes them unique?
- Location, mobility, access and contacts – what makes them unique?
- Recommendations, testimonials and references – what makes them unique?

You'll soon have a clear idea of what your USPs are – create a list, a short description (10–15 words) that encapsulates them and a 150-word profile that sums these up. You'll need this for client pitches and for use in all your marketing efforts. Include powerful ad words such as *you* (to directly communicate with the customer) and highly visual attention-grabbing adjectives. Remember, unique is just that: wholly unlike any other. So, make sure what you are saying is different, inviting and exciting. In any business, identical and samey is boring. Also check that you are not positioning yourself purely as a commodity. Take time to craft a powerful USP that mirrors what your target market wants – and what they may not be getting from other writers.

AWARDS AND SPONSORSHIPS

Every year, a wide variety of trade organisations, publishers, magazines and travel websites run an incredible array of different competitions and awards for writers. Most offer prizes and all benefit from promotion. So by entering you stand a very good chance of winning a prize of monetary value while raising your profile and boosting your credentials to boot. Each and every award and competition has its own set of rules regarding eligibility. Many are open to unpublished writers while others require a published portfolio. Some are run by local libraries or community colleges but you'll also find travel-writing competitions organised by all sorts of commercial concerns, from credit card companies and currency exchanges to tour operator associations. Many of the most successful income-generating freelancers make a point of staying well-informed about competitions and awards all over the globe. Most are able to submit a piece of work they've already written so entering is as quick as filling in a form and sending an email. With thousands of competitions in the UK alone the opportunities for motivated writers with their finger on the pulse are surprisingly diverse. Prizes range from £25 to £3,000 or more – so it pays to stay abreast of new awards and competitions as they are launched. Yet, winning awards isn't all about the cheque: they bring prestige, kudos and respect. Prize-winners will also find that well-run competitions offer excellent PR opportunities. By raising a writer's profile, a competition can lead to more offers of work, both directly and indirectly. They can also enhance your reputation, attract new business propositions and ultimately make you more profitable. Of course, to be in with a chance, the old adage applies: 'you've got to be in it to win it'. The more awards you enter, the greater your chance of success. Many travel writers enter upwards of 15 awards a year, often in countries all over the world.

‘ **WINNING AND GRINNING**

An Expert's View...

'It's BBC Wildlife Magazine *for you.'*

That call sounded the death-knell for my day job. I could hardly take in the news: winner of the Nature Travel Writing Competition 2000. Cue brief gob-smacked silence, then big whoop and inept high fives with mystified colleagues.

Call it fluke or destiny. Either way it was the lucky break that launched my freelance career. I say 'launched'. In fact it took three years of whittling down my hours at the office, from full time to part time to pointless time, before I took the plunge. That prize, though, sowed the seeds. Winning brought me contacts, credibility and – crucially – confidence. I can't pretend it's been a meteoric rise ever since. But once somebody has shown faith in your writing, you dare to believe there'll be others.

Anyway, if all else fails, a free safari can't be bad. ’

Mike Unwin (gemwin@ntlworld.com) writes guidebooks for Bradt Travel Guides and articles for the *Independent* and *Travel Africa*, among many others. Travel, wildlife and Africa are his usual themes – but he'll try anything.

Quality of your work

Of course, to win awards, you need to have the quality of work that can stand up to the scrutiny of experienced judges. Most competitions enlist the help of a team of highly-respected professionals so you will need to be sure that your submission hits the spot. Many writers plan their portfolio of entries with forethought; earmarking potential articles, guidebooks and photographs throughout each year. By keeping a file of exceptional examples of your work in this way, entering awards can be simple and time-efficient – otherwise you're faced with trawling through published material to see what is suitable or good enough. Nothing prevents you from submitting a particularly outstanding piece of work for multiple awards in different regions and countries. Niche writers may also find that they have a real advantage. If you're serious about maximising opportunities it pays to create a spreadsheet of what is upcoming on a year-by-year basis. Include submission deadlines, contact information and ensure you are fully familiar with all the rules because these can change from one year to another.

If the competition requires you to write a specific piece for entry then make sure you take time to read the brief in detail. Many of the larger awards offer a commission as part of the prize, be it photography or writing. This provides unpublished travel writers and photographers with the ideal outcome: a prestigious accolade, some prize money, publicity and a raised profile, together with a published piece of work. Many writers win awards long before they are published. They gain confidence and greater direction from the entry process and the professional feedback and critique they receive. In this respect, awards should be viewed as positive step in commercial sanity, not merely an outlet for vanity. For many writers, hearing 'And the award goes to. . .' before their name, is just the boost in motivation they need in order to keep on plugging away. It lends third-party credibility to what you're doing and can be a much-needed pat on the back.

Awards ceremonies also enable writers to network with commissioning editors. One of the most dazzling is the British Guild of Travel Writers' annual Gala Dinner, an upscale ceremony held annually at a top hotel in London that coincides with the start of World Travel Market (WTM) in November. Another highly-respected annual travel-writing competition is organised by Bradt Travel Guides. Prizes are awarded in conjunction with the *Independent on Sunday* at an event at Stanfords Travel Book Shop in London's Covent Garden.

Unfortunately, there is no central source for details of travel writing awards and competitions, so you'll need to set aside some time to scour the internet for details. It may help to set up a Google Alert to notify you as information is added or updated. Other good sources include the Society of Women Writers and Journalists and British Guild of Travel Writers together with membership organisations and associations (see Appendix 2).

❝ COMPETITIONS COUNT

An Expert's View...

For several years, Bradt Travel Guides – the leading independent travel publisher, best known for guidebooks that take you off the beaten track – has organised an annual travel-writing competition. Entrants are asked to compose an 800-word piece on a specified theme; past themes have included 'Destination Unknown' and 'The

Heart of the City'. Each piece must be drawn from a real-life experience, and have a strong element of travel. Judges are looking for pieces that: adhere closely to the theme; have a good shape and an attention-grabbing opening 'hook'; avoid clichés in painting an imaginative picture; and hold interest throughout.

The competition has proved an enormous success, and regularly attracts over 500 entries. The first prize is a holiday and a commission for a piece in the Independent on Sunday *newspaper. There is also a prize for the best piece by an unpublished writer. The competition usually runs between April and May, with the awards ceremony in July.*

Adrian Phillips is the publishing director at Bradt Travel Guides and the 2006 winner of the British Guild of Travel Writers' 'Guide Book of the Year Award'. He has a PhD in English Literature and writes regularly for national newspapers and magazines (including *The Express, The Independent* and *Wanderlust*). (Visit: www.bradtguides.com)

SPONSORSHIPS

Setting up some sort of sponsorship programme rarely ranks high on the list of a budding travel writers 'to do' list. However, once you've started to secure commissions it may be something that presents itself as part and parcel of your job. By nature, many travel writers are conscientious about journeying responsibly and supporting sustainable tourism models. They often feel compelled to 'give something back' to the communities and places they've encountered along the way. This could be as simple as including details of volunteer projects in an article you're writing about a poverty-stricken region you've visited in India.

However, many writers who spend extended periods in a specific location or who are niche writers specialising in a certain country have an urge to do more. They may volunteer themselves or get involved in a social programme. Or they could set up a UK foundation in order to channel efforts more effectively; utilising contacts and resources at home in order to aid a situation or community in a country that is dear to their heart.

Travel guidebook authors are particularly involved in sponsoring or partnering overseas charity projects. In the months they spend researching a book they become integrated into countries and communities and are often able to identify with the local people. They witness financial hardship and shortfalls in basic healthcare and education. Feeling compelled to be more involved than a casual observer often starts when you're 'on the road'. However, for many writers a determination to 'do something' continues once they're on home soil, slogging away on their manuscript, hunched over a PC.

As keen observers, travel writers are often in a unique and privileged position to fully understand the on-going difficulties faced by isolated communities. They can also find themselves thrust into scenes of untold devastation and social upheaval, such as those who were in Iran when the earthquake of 2003 killed many thousands and destroyed an entire town. Following the tsunami of 2004 – the deadliest in recorded history – many of the travel writers who were in the worst-affected regions threw themselves into helping in any way they could.

Others specialising in African stories have felt compelled to channel their fund-raising efforts into bringing a greater awareness of the widespread suffering caused by the HIV virus.

Over two million Africans die each year while at least 25 million are believed to be infected – figures that are continuing to rise day by day.

Getting involved

Getting involved in helping the countries that you visit is beneficial on many levels. It can strengthen your bond and knowledge of a destination and can help a writer better understand the challenges that country faces. It can also demonstrate a clear commitment to value of a global traveller, not as a passive traveller who ticks off attractions – but as a human who treasures Planet Earth.

It's not just travel writers who are subscribing to the policy of 'giving something back'. Big business, which also makes its money from journeying, is doing the same. Airlines are bringing in vast sums through onboard donation schemes that gather unwanted foreign currency from travellers. And frequent fliers are even handing over their precious air miles to help causes overseas – Virgin Atlantic jet-setters donated enough to help rebuild a school in the Masai Mara game reserve in Kenya. In 15 years, British Airways has raised almost $46 million for UNICEF through its Change for Good initiative. In 2007, funds were also used for emergency relief work in response to the Bangladesh cyclone, the South East Asia floods and the Darfur emergency.

Miles donated through Air France-KLM's frequent flier programme are converted into tickets and sent to charities that help mobilise surgeons, physicians, nurses and foster families for children in medical need in developing countries. The new Travellers Giving Back initiative launched by STI has been created to encourage travellers to donate to charity when booking a holiday.

The Ritz-Carlton hotel chain runs a highly-successful Community Footprints programme, donating over $8.5 million in 2008 alone to charitable organisations close to each of its properties. Staff also volunteered more than 57,000 hours to help out in community projects. So, it's not just travel writers who have their conscience pricked by the way they are able to make money from visiting countries in need.

Deciding on projects

Deciding how to help and what projects to be involved with is a highly personal decision. You may only be able to offer to organise a fund-raising raffle at your local pub or you may decide you've the time to set up a charity or foundation to manage something on a larger scale. You might donate some time to volunteer in some way or you could consider setting aside a percentage of income from articles and books – especially if they are about the country concerned. That you are 'giving something back' is also a valuable USP (see page 122) that clearly demonstrates your values and principles.

More and more publishers are placing considerable importance on responsible travel and all that it entails. So don't view it as crass to promote your responsible travel ethos as a profile-raising opportunity because by conveying your ideals to like-minded clients you are highlighting why you are different. Let them know about the local charities that have benefited from your help and the social programmes that you have sponsored and the gratification you've felt from knowing that you've 'done your bit' to help. Increasingly, travel guide publishers are commissioning taking into account a travel author's commitment to responsible tourism. Editors, too, want to see that a writer has something deeper than a superficial visual impression. So if you're increasingly keen to build some kind of relationship with the country you're visiting and want to remain involved with it after the end or your trip – make a deliberate contribution while you travel and be sure to add it to your USPs.

Once you're involved with the project – be it sponsoring a school in Colombia, sourcing donated art materials to a community project in Senegal, fundraising for housing in Jamaica or starting a volunteer programme in India – take some great photographs and put together some copy about what, where, how and why.

You can then do some (or all) of the following.

- Include it in an email bulletin.

- Add it to your website.

- Send press releases to local, regional, national and trade press.

- Issue press releases to location-specific magazines.

- Send press releases to charity publications with links to the project or destination.

- Send press releases to local and regional TV and radio.

- Issue press releases to tour operators with links to the project or destination.

◆ Send press releases to the tourist boards with links to the project or destination.

◆ Notify your publisher's press office (they may post something on the website and engage their own publicity machine to further promote the cause).

◆ Post it on Facebook, Twitter or other social networking sites.

◆ Get it printed as postcards for an eye-catching mailshot.

Try to secure talks or public-speaking events so that you can spread the word about the project, because it will help widen the net for donations and offers of support. It will also further demonstrate your commitment and understanding of your niche market and to responsible travel as a whole.

It may also be possible to add a 'donate now' feature to your website – for goods, services and volunteers – together with information on how people can help.

If you are a member of a trade organisation, let the secretariat know what you are doing. It may be possible for them to support your activities in some way, such as a dinner fund-raiser or an evening of talks and presentations to your peers that is dedicated to your project. With well-planned co-ordination you may be able to get the Tourist Office on board to supply local foods from the country or region – that way it can be a showcase event for the project, the association and the destination that further cements your travel ethos and determination to 'give something back'.

Choosing a charity or programme to support

Deciding where to focus your energies can be a challenge as there are so many programmes and charities in dire need of your time and hard-earned cash. Should you support the environmental group that is fighting to save the Darien jungle, the community association that battling drugs in Riohacha or the children's charity crying out for help for its several hundred orphans in Shanghai?

Most travel writers pick the charities and volunteer programmes they support from first-hand experiences of their mission. Through travel, you are more likely to find groups whose purpose matters to you and where you feel you can truly get involved. Donors and volunteers can give so much more than financial income. But here are some other tips to help make sure your efforts are well spent.

◆ **Give to groups you know and relate to**
  Knowing the organisation and identifying and understanding the work that it does will give you the motivation to get fully involved. It will also enable you to promote its values with confidence that offers of support and donations will be put to good use.

◆ **Make sure the charity is the one you think it is**
  Check that the charity is a well-respected organisation – it doesn't need to be large and internationally recognised, some of the smaller programmes are just as well run. Don't assume you know the group or what it does – ask questions and spend time with the organisers to experience it at first hand.

◆ **Make sure you understand the group's work**
  Charities tackle problems in different ways. For example,

groups that try to lower the rate of teenage pregnancy in Africa may do so by teaching sex education, by promoting sexual abstinence or by offering programmes that aim to build self-esteem among teenage girls. There are many ways to approach a problem, so take time to fully understand the exact aims and business model of the programme. Ask for details of past projects, the history of the charity and the background of its founder and be sure to meet the people it has helped.

♦ **Ask what it needs**
Don't assume that a charity is in need of financial aid because many programmes, such as those involved in medical services, require volunteer professionals, equipment and supplies above all else.

♦ **Find out about specific campaigns**
For example, the charity may have an upcoming push to train its local community in a particular trade. This may be easier to focus your efforts on – you may be able to source specific skills or equipment easier than conducting a wider, broader effort.

♦ **Volunteering opportunities**
Establish how well set up the charity is for volunteering. For example, does it have accommodation for visiting volunteers; can it feed them day-to-day? Also, ask if there are any specific types of volunteers it needs, for example language experts, professionals or people who can provide labour or farming expertise.

❛ GIVING SOMETHING BACK

An Expert's View...

Travelling has taken me to places of extreme poverty. I have witnessed impoverished peoples who are underfed and unable to access medical help; children working to support their families; slums and shanty towns. I've always felt as a travel writer promoting tourism, I have some responsibility to inform tourists of these issues. I've found guidebook publishers are not only impressed with in-depth knowledge of local issues, but quite often demand it. Less space is available for these concerns in holiday sections of travel magazines and newspaper print. But in this case, I have tried to pitch features to other genres; travel writing is not limited to hotel reviews! Researching local issues immerses the writer in communities and culture, which I've found enables writing to stand out from superficial pieces. Helping out with local environment or conservation projects, for example, earns you trust and respect and stories you may not have encountered otherwise – keep every contact you make, they could be useful for future features. For me, good travel journalism subtly shifts from the holiday pleasures consumers expect, to integrate social and political dimensions, multifaceted cultural practices and colour. 🟊

Freelance writer and author Heloise Crowther specialises in global issues and travel and has worked for publications from guidebooks to newspapers, in the UK and Latin America. (Visit: www.globaljourno.com)

TIME MANAGEMENT

Effectively managing punishing schedules, conflicting deadlines and the expectations of editors and publishers is a key part of a travel writer's lot. In an ideal world, work would flow in at an easy, measured pace allowing easy weekly scheduling. However, the reality is that after an empty week, a whole slew of jobs will come in all at once with the exactly the same deadline. So, you're faced with a seven-day week and umpteen articles to write, causing you to wonder in a panic: how on earth am I going to fit it all in?

Using a project management system will help you manage particularly heavy writing schedules. By inputting deadlines and milestones, you'll be able to clearly see what conflicts there are. It will also allow you to manage your sales in advance to fill up gaps and maximise revenue streams effectively. However, even without a sophisticated system, it is possible to stay ahead of the game.

Creating a simple Word document or utilising a proper business diary (with a daily, monthly and yearly planner) will enable you to plan, juggle and co-ordinate projects so that you can clearly see what is what. Be diligent in this time management: in the deadline-driven publishing world there is little room for sloppy service delivery. Miss a deadline and you are highly unlikely to be used again by the commissioning editor, who has been sweating and biting their nails whilst growing increasingly more frustrated and angry by the minute.

Reliability is the cornerstone of travel writing. Publishing schedules tend to be immovable forces, so it is imperative that you view the deadline as such. Most of the most successful income-generating freelancers have time management down to a fine art. They elongate their working day, up the ante when it comes to pre-planning and are able to switch between projects with proficient ease to deliver high-quality work – bang on time.

Poor time-management indicators

By choosing to adopt poor time-management habits and badly prioritise what's important, you are in effect creating a below-par return on investment. Some indicators of poor time management are as follows.

♦ Constant rushing (e.g. between meetings or tasks).

♦ Frequent lateness (e.g. attending meetings, seeing clients or meeting deadlines).

♦ Low productivity, energy and motivation (e.g. 'I can't seem to get worked up about anything').

♦ Frustration (e.g. 'I'm pulled in a million different directions').

♦ Impatience (e.g. 'Where the heck is that information I've asked him for? He's holding me back from getting on with my work').

♦ Chronic vacillation between alternatives (e.g. 'I've been scratching my head for weeks over this. I don't know which way to jump').

♦ Difficulty setting and achieving goals (e.g. 'I'm not sure what my focus is or what is expected of me').

♦ Procrastination (i.e. continually putting off starting a task or activity. This may occur because you fear failing to do a good job or baulk at the effort required).

Perfectionism and an unrealistic, uncompromising pursuit of exceptionally high standards can be another form of poor time management. By working slowly to avoid making any mistakes or becoming totally preoccupied with a point of detail we can often be stalling other projects for no real reason. It is important not to become bogged down in too much of the nitty-gritty that prevents us from managing our schedule. Feeling overwhelmed by your workload can come as a direct result of not knowing when a job is finished – when you feel compelled to continually check details when it isn't necessary.

Count the cost

It can be scary sometimes to calculate just how much wasted time can cost us. On the basis that you are working 250 × 8 hour days a year it can be frightening how easily time slips by – at a price.

♦ For every hour you spend fussing about without purpose the cost could be as much as £30.

♦ Every morning you spend catching up on your personal administration because you are poorly organised could cost you £90.

♦ A day spent sitting in the wrong meeting could cost around £200.

If you were paying out cash for all of this, you would certainly evaluate your expenditure and refocus your priorities – so it is well worth keeping it in check.

You can see now how your poor time management could be costing you dearly and that's only in financial terms – but you can easily make impactful changes:

♦ by saving five minutes a day, you will increase your productivity by 2.6 full days;

♦ by saving 30 minutes a day, you will increase your productivity by 15.63 full days;

◆ by saving one hour a day, you will increase your productivity by 31.25 full days.

Every travel writer moans that they 'don't have enough time' to achieve what they set out to – but by managing our schedules we can create it by the smallest changes to our daily routines.

❛ PUNCTUALITY PAYS

An Expert's View...

In my experience, editors will commission further work from you if you deliver your copy punctually, so managing your time is of the utmost importance. When I receive a commission, I divide the number of words by the number of weeks available. Depending on the amount of research I have to do, I can see immediately if I need to ask for an extension in advance. Editors don't mind if you ask for an extra week or two when you sign the contract on a book, because this is when they begin their planning, whereas asking for more time towards the end is a big no-no. Afterwards I keep a calendar on the wall with the words I need to complete every week marked clearly, so that I have a clear view of my progress at any one time. Oh, and I leave at least one day per week free for revisions and corrections. ❜

Travel author and writer John Malathronas was born in Athens but has lived in London for most of his life. He is a Member of the British Guild of Travel Writers and contributes to a host of magazines worldwide and is the author of *Brazil: Life, Blood and Soul, Rainbow Diary: A Journey in the New South Africa* and *Singapore Swing* (published by Summersdale). (Visit: www.scroll.demon.co.uk/spaver.htm)

Depending on the publishing outlet, sometimes there may be room to negotiate an extended deadline – especially if meeting it is an impossible task. You are unlikely to be cut any slack on daily newspapers where the pace is fast, furious and time-precious. However, on monthly titles or bi-annual magazines you may be able to squeeze an extra day or so to ease the pressure. Always discuss this up-front with the commissioning editor. Never assume submitting copy late is acceptable – it rarely is. Editors need to be able to rely on their contributors in every sense – not just in the quality of work you produce but how and when you produce it. Remember that they are part of a process that involves other time-sensitive departments with their own pressing deadline demands. So, should you be able to negotiate a revised date to submit your work, stick to it. Otherwise, the editor will have egg on their face – and your name will be mud.

Travel guidebooks and book publishers may ask you to set your own deadline, after which they will set the marketing wheels in motion. A date will be set for publication and ultimately for sale. Production schedules will be finalised, printing will be organised and every part of the project management process put into place. It is therefore very important not to quote a date 'off the cuff', but to consider possible constraints and anticipate scheduling conflicts. If you are new to guidebook work, ask your publisher for advice on time scheduling – then add in a contingency for peace for mind. It is better to deliver early or hit the deadline with comfort than to promise an ultra-impressive timescale that you haven't a hope of meeting.

Other book projects will have a set-in-stone schedule that leaves little room for manoeuvre. Normally, in this instance, the commission phase comes after the print and production dates

have been finalised. You will be offered the job on the basis that
you can fulfil the project to meet the deadline. In these
circumstances, the timescale is rarely open for debate – it may be
possible to extend it for an extra few days or so but nothing more.
As you'll be asked to sign a contract that confirms your
acceptance of these terms, it is important that you evaluate your
schedule before you say an emphatic 'yes please' to the
proposition. Calculate the time required for the project and put it
into your time-management schedule to see if it is do-able first. If
you simply can't get the work to fit in, then you know you have a
problem. It is important to raise this ahead of the contract stage
as, once you have signed the deal, you will be legally bound to
deliver on time – or face the consequences.

Tips for time management

If you find it hard to grapple with multiple projects, then take
time to assess your scheduling. Ask yourself: 'Am I a time waster?'
and analyse how you can better manage your day. Plot what you
do and how you do it. If there is an imbalance that is affecting
your work rate, take steps to address it.

Writing is a solitary profession that requires discipline from
freelancers on the road. Create a simple way to track your time,
using project management software, a diary or planner. This time
log should be adhered to religiously, so be sure to keep it up to
date with all the activities you perform – and how long they take.

On a daily basis, plan your day to enable goals and milestones to
be met. Add every commission and every research project. Every
day set aside time for sales and marketing. Include deadlines and
other immovable dates (such as meetings, networking events and

travel days) to allow a planning log that takes into account overlap and conflicts.

Be honest about your writing rate and be aware of your own working patterns and behaviours. Are you easily distracted? Are there certain things that are preventing you from focusing on great writing? Look at ways in which you can approach your day to make it more business focused and time efficient. It may be that you are better suited to writing at certain times of the day. Marketing and sales activities may be more productive at specific times of the week.

Explore ways to add extra 'days' to your week during a particularly busy period. For example, if you need an extra day, simply add 1 ½ hours to each day of your working week ($5 \times 1.5 = 7\frac{1}{2}$ hours), if you need two extra days, add three (3×15 hours $= 2$ days at 7½ hours each). These short-time measures can be an effective solution to time management conflicts. Control your time rather than allowing time to control you.

Assess upcoming 'gaps' in your working schedule and reconcile these against your financial goals. If there is a shortfall in revenue, start taking steps to generate additional work and income. Do this as soon as possible (by checking your work log regularly you'll be able to identify down-time well ahead of schedule), as it may take a few weeks for your marketing efforts to bear fruit.

Don't put too much pressure on yourself – take the time to get the balance right. You need to be a workhorse to make money from travel writing, but you'll be a far better writer and have a more focused business mind if you don't feel over-burdened, overstretched and approaching burn-out. Schedule down-time to rejuvenate your creative juices and, when you've hit your financial goals, book a few days off to appreciate the flexibility that freelancing can bring.

❛ISOLATION, OLD TRACKSUITS AND LONG HOURS

An Expert's View...

Even I need to remind myself that there's a writing part to travel writing. Yet it is this important second component – the writing – that takes up far more time than the travelling itself. Writing is an isolating occupation that brings out one's worst tendencies, such as wearing old tracksuits with holes in them. The freelance part also makes time management so vital as it means you have to do so much else other than travelling and writing. If a parcel needs to be sent, you have to go to the post office and stand in the queue. If the computer throws a tantrum, you're the one who'll have to soothe it. There is no post room or IT department. No switchboard operator. The time that these administrative tasks swallow is quite horrifying.

It's often said that freelance work is feast or famine: you're either swamped by work – or there's nothing. However, my freelance life is almost always busy because, even if I'm not writing, there is so much else to be done. Stories need pitching and there are PRs to meet (and yes, knowing people personally does help), tax returns to be filed and photos to be edited. Then, of course, there are the endless streams of little, demanding administrative tasks. None of these jobs is directly fee-earning – but all are an important part of the job.

A freelance life is a wonderful one. You have absolute freedom. You can focus on those areas of your profession that interest you the most – and you don't have a boss. But almost every freelancer I know taps away at their computer evenings and weekends – not poor time management but more simply a matter of long hours.

Polly Evans is an award-winning journalist who writes regularly for publications including the *Independent on Sunday*, *Wanderlust*, *Condé Nast Traveller*, and the *Sunday Times Travel Magazine*. She is also the author of five narrative travel books as well as *Yukon: The Bradt Travel Guide*. (Visit www.pollyevans.com)

DEALING WITH REJECTION

Every writer gets rejections – it is part and parcel of pitching. It is simply not possible to win a pitch every time. The question becomes how to interpret them, and what to do next. It is easy to feel dejected when you receive a 'thanks but no thanks' email – but it is important not to be down-hearted. An editor may reject your idea for a multitude of reasons, so you should never confuse a 'no thanks' with a 'never in your wildest dreams'. They are simply saying the story isn't right for them at that particular time, so don't take it as a scathing appraisal of your writing talent. Take the rejection on the chin and use it to your positive advantage whilst remembering that it is likely to mean one or more of the following reasons.

- They have just accepted a similar story.
- They just recently ran a similar story.
- They have a huge stack of commissions in a slush pile (that'll last them several months)
- The editor is grumpy that day.

Writers who are dedicated marketers of their work will find they get many rejections – because of the rate at which they pitch for upcoming work or suggest new ideas. It stands to reason that when you pitch ten ideas a year you're never going to experience more than ten rejections. However, once you start pitching over several hundred times a year, your chances of being turned down will increase.

The important factor to focus on is the percentage of pitches that are rejected – once you know this, you can work on actively improving your success rate. To this end, it is important to keep a record of all your marketing activities so that you can log what is working – and what is failing to make the grade. Evaluating your pitching success rate is paramount to maximising your revenue stream. Never let your ego get in the way of self-improvement in this area – it will only hurt your bottom line. Approach rejection in an intelligent way with a business focus – after all, every customer has a right to buy from whom they please. Yet there are many, many factors that influence a consumer's decision. Don't make rash assumptions and never write a potential client off simply because they said 'no' once – the only person losing out in this instance is you. Consider the following.

Success as a writer often depends more on intelligent persistence than on raw talent. Learn from mistakes, figure out what you're doing wrong, and work hard to change it. Many writers give up after one rejection – despite having incredible talent. However, others – possibly with less creative talent – will plug away solidly while shouldering the rejections. It is these persistent, marketing-focused, resilient freelance writers who often gain the most commissions.

Rejected ideas and pitches often have nothing to do with writing merit – as many editors will testify. So many trivial factors determine which articles or books get published. Rejections can be a result of budgetary constraints, political in-fighting and scheduling issues. In short, rejections shouldn't be taken too seriously, unless they are specific critiques.

Plan for rejection before it happens. As you wait for responses from your first batch of pitches, gather a list of editors as 'Phase B'. Should ideas be rejected, send them out again to a fresh set of contacts (the 'Phase B' editors). In just a few short hours, you can transform disappointment into hope – and, ultimately success.

Should an editor proffer specific criticism, regard it as a gift. Thank them for the time they've taken to critique your work – whether you agree or not. Even if you're offended, take a deep breath and avoid emailing back a response in a tantrum. Remain neutral about the comments – it's about your work (your product) not about you.

If a pitch simply isn't working, then take the time to rejection-proof it for a fresh campaign. Incorporate any specific feedback that may be the key to a better rate of success. Does your pitch lack warmth or passion? If it does, then make conveying a clear expression of your enthusiasm a part of your primary goal. It is easy to lose this vital component when pitching for business, so upping your success rate can often be as simple as giving it an injection of zeal.

Evaluate any patterns of rejection: are they happening with the same client repeatedly, or do they relate to a pitch made on a certain day? Does one style of approach (email) work better than another (letter)? Or does the first week of each month reap better rewards than any other time? Consult your marketing log, learn what works, and build this into your work schedule in order to maximise those winning pitches.

Don't allow yourself to be down in the dumps. Wallowing in self-doubt and rejection serves no positive purpose. Consider your favourite movie, best-loved book and all-time cherished song if the talent behind these had simply given up at the first rejection it would have been ridiculous. So, don't let rejection stop you.

SURVIVING A DOWNTURN

From a business perspective, whether the economy is in a recession or not is somewhat immaterial. Managing a small business can be difficult even during the best of times – and travel writing is no exception. In the midst of an economic downturn, however, it becomes more important for travel writers to focus on what they are doing as motivation can become a determining factor between staying afloat and going under. Yet, whether we are in good times or bad, we all need to know how to steer the business back to 'safe harbour'. An important part of this navigation is an ability to focus on the reality of a situation without subscribing to the hype.

Even in the worst economic downturns, many freelance writers survive and thrive. So never let the mood of gloom and despondency cloud your goals. Despite ailing economies, magazines continue to publish, websites continue to attract traffic and newspapers are sold all over the world. Budgets may be squeezed but freelancers can still find work – they just may need to be more entrepreneurial and creative in their approach. Ingenuity and flexibility are valuable skills in a deflated publishing market when the brightest ideas and more imaginative pitches shine out. A downturn does not mean that opportunities have ceased. Editors are still commissioning although maybe not in the freewheeling kind of way of the last few years. Just like any business feeling the pinch, a travel writer will need to adapt to the changing needs of a depressed economy. Companies across the world invest considerable time in researching how they can ride out the storm. In order to meet your own financial goals, you will need to do so too.

There is much talk about how small businesses can protect themselves from the worst of a downturn. 'Recession proofing' is a prudent exercise whenever you start a business. Many economic slumps happen without warning so being proactive to plan for this eventuality is the key. In 2008, studies by the think tank Tenon Forum revealed that four in ten (38%) of small business set-ups had no plans in place to address risks associated with a downturn in trade. It cited having a 'Plan B' as the most important contingency. It also urged small businesses not to be tempted to slash prices in order to boost sales. This is especially important for freelance travel writers who can often over-react to weakened market conditions and fail to make the distinction between being competitive and giving profits away. Sure, it may be a time for publishers to tighten their belts – but this doesn't necessarily mean that it will be at your expense. Don't automatically offer reduced prices or discounts but try to stick to your normal fee structure. If you do need to restructure tariffs, be sure to offset these by exploring new ways to ease your tax cashflow position. By managing late payments sensibly and negotiating keener banking conditions you should be able to balance the books.

Yet, on the whole, freelance travel writers are a frugal bunch used to working and living lean. Headlines may scream about layoffs, business failures and closures but for writers the economy has always been uncertain. Many writers, out of sheer necessity, have developed a wide-ranging set of survival skills that can serve them well when the hard times hit home. Inside every writer is a hidden juggler, who is good at keeping enough work trickling while sailing the high seas seeking out new projects. We are resourceful and adept at making our craft pay the bills.

Traditionally, publicity (advertising and marketing) is one of the first activities to be hit by an economic slump. Many small businesses feel that this is an easy expense to trim down on when times are bad. On the flip side, you could use the opportunity to gain more of the market share if your rivals decide to pull back on their marketing spend. This is a good time to work harder on your marketing to compensate for any shrinkage in your potential client base.

A recession is a time when you need to keep your own customer base happy. It is also a good time to get the best out of your own suppliers. Your bargaining power will increase during rocky times and you may well be able to secure discounts on products and services (such as stationery, computer peripherals, travel insurance and medical supplies). Take a view of the medium-term state of the economy and try to lock in discounted deals for longer periods, so you benefit not only now but also when the economy improves.

One of the worst approaches to a recession is shut down hopes and goals. A downturn shouldn't mean that you need to curtail your business vision. Your ethos, standards and aspirations should still stand strong. In fact, in a recession they should be strengthened. Developing writers should keep honing their skills while those with their eye on their next great book should continue on their path.

However, it is paramount for travel writers to review how they're working in order to protect their profit margins and aspirations. Be sure to:

- identify and bolster any business shortcomings. Are you operating effectively?

- reinforce your USPs – let your uniqueness shine out;

- up your marketing activity – grab every opportunity to sell your services;

- broaden your horizons – are there untapped markets you could explore?

- stay curious – a downturn is no time to shut down your own thinking. In fact, it is time to open it up;

- ask questions to establish if/how clients are changing their business model (you can then build a proposal and pitches against this shift);

- rein in your expenditure unless it is a justifiable part of your income-generating goals. Set expenses against commissions and scrutinise your bottom line;

- manage your cashflow and find the best deals on bank cards and currency. Look into the best savings options for contingency reserves and tax payments;

- approach all orphan clients (editors that used to use you but whose commissions have tailed off) to utilise all potential 'soft' sales contacts;

- avoid letting the gloominess of a depressed economy curb your enthusiasm – your passion for your work and keenness to win pitches should be evident in all that you do;

- seek out countries least affected by the downturn as a potential market;

- explore new mediums to work in that are least affected by the slump;

- seek out specialist titles that represent sectors least affected by the recession;

- pitch unique, interesting ideas that are fitting for a time of economic depression. Avoid the obvious to focus on original well thought out story angles. You may be able to turn the slump into a specialist subject.

Brace yourself for the bounce

Remember, every depressed economy eventually recovers, and travel writers who can pre-empt the bounce-back have a clear business advantage. Planning for better days is no easy task when the economic outlook is so uncertain. However, it is important to take the time to understand what is actually happening in the publishing world in regard to planning, budgets and future projects. Get your timing right and you'll be able to reap the rewards of pitching ahead of the pack. Don't get bogged down with the hearsay, consult the experts in the financial media. Then put a plan in motion in order to maximise the opportunities and new-found confidence that a recovered economy brings.

Tips to take advantage of an economic bounce

- Manage cashflow to ensure you are in the best position possible to capitalise on improving conditions.

- Develop skills that could enhance future collaborations and projects – this is the ideal time to 'talent upgrade' yourself to maximise what you can offer.

- Start looking into forming strategic partnerships that will pay off further down the road.

- Stay up to date with travel conditions, industry updates and legislation to ensure you enter the bounce fully primed with pertinent knowledge and industry insight.

- Investigate new technologies or new working models that could give you the edge when the recovery hits full bounce.

- Maximise your client relationships to ensure you are at the forefront of their mind. Invest time in meetings, lunches and networking to ensure your contacts book is full – and up to date.

- Consider the possibility of new services – a bounce-back can be an excellent business climate in which to launch something new or visionary.

Be aware that many of your major competitors may not have
survived the economic slump. While other travel writers will have
undoubtedly slipped off the radar, be sure to publicise the fact
that you are still around. Reinforce your mission statement (see
page 120) and demonstrate that you remain committed to the field
of travel writing. That you have stuck around and survived the
rigours of a recession will say a lot about your determination,
stamina and grit. Also that you were quick, flexible and fluid
enough to turn the demands of a downturn into a business
opportunity – no mean feat. Anyone can dip in and out of a
career when the good times roll yet it takes a different breed of
freelancer to ride the economic storm.

SURVIVING A DOWNTURN

When times get tough, the natural human instinct is to retreat to
rudimentary levels of behaviour and protect one's basic individual
needs. For most people, this means cutting costs and seeing out
the storm while praying they can survive on good reputation alone.
Of course this may be possible, but most of us will need to find
ways to continue to build trade. However bad the economy, it is
important not to freeze your marketing budget during a recession
because this will hamper the very activities that can drum up extra
trade.

Online or offline, marketing is a crucial tool in creating lasting
business connections. Utilising your website to its full potential is
an inexpensive way to boost your profile and generate sales. It also
offers travel writers a way to instantly track exactly how much
traffic and how many enquiries they are generating, allowing them
to dump or change what's not working and maximise what
is. Consider adding advice, white papers, risk-free trials, interesting
downloads and podcasts, audio testimonials, case studies and

guarantees. Interactive websites allow businesses to chart who is visiting their website, so try creative, inventive and engaging ways to encourage potential customers to pass on their contacts online.

Try testing the following to see if it works for you.

- Google Adwords.
- Search engine optimisation.
- Pepping up your website's content.
- Incentives for website traffic to leave their email address.
- Email marketing.
- Adding a blog.
- Using audio and video clips.
- Creating affiliate relationships and joint ventures for income.

5

Expanding Your Market

❛ *The traveller sees what he sees. The tourist sees what he has come to see.* ❜

G K Chesterton

WRITING FOR OVERSEAS MARKETS

By its very definition, travel writing has few geographic borders. We can write wherever we are in the world and seek out publishers anywhere on the planet. Just as the publishing world evolves continually, so does the scope of travel writing. Technology allows every freelance travel writer to work from every part of the globe. As this technology advances, so must travel writers – especially those keen to maximise their publishing options.

To explore new streams of potential income, travel writers should be prepared to cover new ground. Even in recent years, there have been huge changes in the way writers make their living. These often require them to form a deeper bond with their computers to seek out clients in foreign lands. With nimble dexterity they switch between different language styles and format requirements while juggling a dozen or so time differences – across five continents.

The internet allows us a vast window on the world and is often a travel writer's greatest asset when it comes to exploring new markets. Not only does it allow us to research new areas of work but it also enables us to work anywhere – which is of paramount importance to travel writers constantly on the move. Wherever we are, it provides a communicative link to our clients – ensuring we can deliver the same level of service as if we were based a half-hour journey away.

If you, like so many others, pay little attention to the internet when it comes to actually getting published, you may want to consider the following advantages to writing for the online market. With email we can communicate with speed between editors and publishers thousands of miles apart. We can conduct online conferencing using shared, inexpensive technology, and whizz files, photographs, videos and audio clips around the world in less time than it takes to lick a stamp.

Writers with a global outlook will methodically target outlets in different countries and cities in order to pursue every possible lead – using just a web browser and an email address. If you are restricted by linguistic limitations (i.e. you can only write in English) start by making a target list of English-speaking nations.

All countries in which English is the official language are listed opposite.

English as an international language
According to language experts, English is on its way to becoming the world's unofficial international language. Mandarin (Chinese) is spoken by more people, but English is now the most widespread of the world's languages. Half of all business deals are conducted in English. Two thirds of all scientific papers are written in

American Samoa
Anguilla
Antigua and
   Barbuda
Australia
Barbados
Belize
Bermuda
Botswana
British Virgin
   Islands
Cameroon
Canada
Cayman Islands
Christmas Island
Cook Islands
Dominica
Falkland Islands
Ghana
Gibraltar
Grenada
Guam
Guernsey
Guyana
Hong Kong
India
Ireland
Isle of Man
Jamaica

Jersey
Kenya
Kiribati
Lesotho
Liberia
Madagascar
Malawi
Malta
Marshall Islands
Mauritius
Micronesia
Montserrat
Namibia
Nauru
New Zealand
Nigeria
Niue
Norfolk Island
Northern Mariana
   Islands
Pakistan
Palau
Papua New Guinea
Philippines
Pitcairn Islands
Puerto Rico
Rwanda
Saint Kitts and
   Nevis

Saint Lucia
Saint Vincent and
   the Grenadines
Samoa
Sierra Leone
Singapore
Solomon Islands
South Africa
Sudan
Swaziland
Tanzania
The Bahamas
The Gambia
Tokelau
Tonga
Trinidad and
   Tobago
Turks and Caicos
Tuvalu
Uganda
UK
United Arab
   Emirates (UAE)
USA
US Virgin Islands
Vanuatu
Zambia
Zimbabwe

Countries in which English is the official language.

English. Over 70% of all post is written and addressed in English. Most international tourism, aviation and diplomacy are conducted in English. All of these activities are reflected in the number for English-language magazines, books and newspapers. The list on page 161 isn't a comprehensive run-down of every English speaking region. For example it doesn't include the Colombian isle Providencia, Senegal or Brunei. So, to explore every possible opportunity conduct your own research to add nations where English is dominant or widely spoken – this list continues to evolve over time.

To look for the publishing opportunities within English-speaking countries, use the following as sources of information in your target regions:

- British High Commission;
- British Embassy;
- British Consulate;
- British Council;
- www.metagrid.com (4,500 magazines listed worldwide);
- www.world-newspapers.com (lists all English-language newspapers around the world);
- publishing associations;
- authors' societies;
- writers' circles;
- travel writing associations;
- journalism associations;
- freelance networking sites.

❝ ONLINE, ANYWHERE IN THE WORLD

An Expert's View...

Much less time is dedicated to reading content online than to the luxury afforded to browsing a printed format, so your messages about the themes and destinations within a travel piece have to be made super-clear within the first sentence.

You will be lucky to keep people beyond the first few paragraphs if they are not getting the feel of the piece straightaway and deciding if it is for them. In addition, the perception is that search engines may only scan the first 200 words anyway, hooking into key travel words and places, so the more obvious you can make these the better, without it making it read as a blatant plea for SEO (Search Engine Optimisation).

Replicating printed travel feature content online will not always work. The online travel sections of the quality nationals have separate teams for web and the paper and whilst they do cross-pollinate – and it is useful to find a back catalogue online – it is always worth considering them as separate people to pitch.

◆ *While you may dedicate much time to creating clever puns for headlines in print, these will be lost on search engines, so to get traffic to the site, the tendency is to be more obvious in captioning and headlining.*

◆ *Quick trends and lists – sorry, but this is one place where travel's fascination with Top 5s/10s of everything really does work – are always great fodder, especially original/well-timed ones with events/themes.*

◆ *The chance for the site visitor to interact with opinion on the piece is increasingly important – witness the phenomenal growth of TripAdvisor and the reason for the launch of Ultra.travel in September 2009 as a place where high-end travellers can visit to inspire and be inspired, hooked in by quality travel features and ideas.*

There has been a move towards paying writers per click-through on the copy, but this can just turn into a situation of plugging places for the sake of the click-through-rate (CTR). Genuinely interested travellers will still always want to read fascinating travellers' tales – albeit shorter ones - and real tips to help their trip planning. **)**

April Hutchinson is launch managing editor of Ultra.travel, a UGC site for high-end travellers, partnered by Cunard, Jumeirah and ITC Classics.

Pitching ideas

For personal introductions and the inside scoop, try posting requests for information and pleas for help on writer blog sites. However, most writers will find that by putting together a database of potential publishing outlets they are well equipped to pitch. If you've got a decent portfolio of work you may also be able to secure representation in certain countries. However you piece together your 'hit list' you'll need to remain mindful that not all English is the same. George Bernard Shaw was credited with the quip 'England and America are two countries separated by a common language' – and it is as important for writers to appreciate the differences as it is for them to understand the similarities. Writers should also be aware of the following issues, when pitching ideas and submitting samples of their work.

◆ **Cultural sensitivity** There is little point in pitching a piece on the vineyards of Chablis to a Islamic nation, so to avoid submitting ideas that may cause offence it is important to be aware of what is acceptable – and what's not. For example, an article on the Falkland Islands will certainly produce a frosty response from a publisher in Argentina. China is sensitive to references to Taiwan, Hong Kong or Macao that suggest that they are countries. In Japan, a feature article that focuses on the Top 4 Golf Resorts, or a narrative that uses the number four as a running metaphor, is unlikely to nurture a positive response – as it holds the meaning of death.

◆ **Globalisation of style** Avoid slang, jargon, humour, sarcasm, colloquialisms and metaphors. For example, use 'estimate' instead of 'in the ballpark'. Do not use Latin abbreviations and avoid negative constructions and ambiguity. Use an appropriate and consistent tone. Avoid using words in multiple grammatical categories (verb, noun, adjective). In English, many words can change their grammatical category. In most other languages, the same word cannot be a verb, a noun and an adjective.

◆ **Spelling and word differences** In some cases the variations are simply a fiddly annoyance, requiring a language check to ensure words such as draught (draft), programme (program), centre (center), colour (color) and cheque (check) are spelt correctly for the target nation. However, objects often have different names, a point of some confusion. For example, an 'automobile' in America has a 'hood' and a 'trunk' while a 'car' in the UK and Australia has a 'bonnet' and a 'boot'. In the extreme cases, the differences can be rather dramatic. A project costing 'one billion' yen may seem rather reasonable in America (a little under $10 million) but outrageously expensive in Singapore (a thousand times more) because the word 'billion' has two different meanings (one thousand million or one million million) depending on where it is used.

- **Idiomatic expressions** Writers often use idiomatic expressions to engage with the reader more naturally in a friendly tone. However, the meanings of such expressions can be difficult to fathom in countries where such idiomatic terms aren't used. Furthermore, idiomatic expressions can be time sensitive – a clever play on words that can easily become a cliché a year down the line.

- **Political correctness** Terms that have derogatory, objectionable, sexual or racial connotations now were often used in everyday language in the past. To avoid using an expression that can appear innocent in one country but may be offensive in another, it is important to be language aware. For example, *Darkie* toothpaste, a popular brand in Asia, changed its name to *Darlie* because of its racial undertones.

❛ HAVE LAPTOP, WILL TRAVEL

An Expert's View...

Ten months ago I arrived in South America, armed with travel-writing experience and a laptop. I started off by selling features as I moved around the continent and then secured a guidebook project that allowed me a long stint in Buenos Aires. My intention is to keep on working here for UK-based publications. These days so much of industry functions via email. Editors want you to deliver good copy on time, but it really doesn't matter where you are when you press that 'send' button. The distance is rarely a problem. For half of the year, the time difference is just two hours, which is barely noticeable. When that rises to four hours, a little more forethought is needed to catch people on the phone, but it's certainly still manageable.

The main problem is ensuring you don't fall out of sight and out of mind, especially when you're no longer able to do the occasional in-house shift or go to industry events. However, online forums and networking sites, such as Twitter, have proved a revelation for keeping in touch and making new contacts. I know I won't make my fortune doing what I'm doing, but I'm confident I can fund a comfortable lifestyle. And if that changes, I'll simply pack my bag again and move on.

Freelance travel writer Vicky Baker is currently based in Buenos Aires. She is the editor of *Time Out Perfect Places Argentina & Uruguay* and writes a travel blog (www.goinglocaltravel.com)

Appreciating cultural sensitivities

Cultural sensitivities also come into play in how you market your business. For example, portraying yourself as a young, fresh and innovative writing talent may not 'sell' in cultures that respect age and longevity. Your logo and corporate identity (see page 97) may also need to be adjusted for overseas markets. Colours, shapes and graphics have differing social, religious and cultural meanings across the world. Photographs should also be selected carefully – pictures may speak a thousand words but they can also say the wrong thing in a foreign country. Take time to understand the cultural implications of your marketing message to ensure that it doesn't have any potential for negative feedback or offence.

Consider the following when launching a marketing campaign overseas.

♦ **Find the common ground** Start by understanding your target customer, their country, their needs, their values and their culture. Take the time to do this for every country in which you plan to pitch ideas.

♦ **Be relevant** Tailor your communications, ideas and service pledges to fit within the social mores of the local culture – it will go a long way to demonstrating that you are committed to the way *they* do business.

♦ **Impact without insult** Certain headings, taglines and titles work globally as attention-grabbers, while others do not. To have global appeal, avoid snappy, snazzy wording and acronyms – they risk baffling the reader and can even insult.

♦ **Website imagery** If you're encouraging overseas clients to visit your website, consider the photographs it contains. Your publicity shot may work well with liberal London publishers but exposed shoulders and arms may not be the most appropriate image to use elsewhere. Similarly, bare legs, feet and ankles may offend.

♦ **Do your homework** Gen up on market trends in the countries you are targeting. Study the way in which the media present the kind of work that you propose to pitch. Familiarise yourself with the kinds of articles that publishers want. Try to obtain several editions of titles that look particularly promising, because hands-on research of what editors commission is often essential to long-term success.

♦ **Be accessible** Make sure your potential clients know that you are as easily accessible as a local writer. Tell them they can contact you at any time. Don't outline the negatives of your remote location and the time differences – highlight the ease with which you serve your overseas clients and the service you arc able to provide. Market your Skype contacts (including the possibility of online conferencing), email address (mentioning that you are reliably online each day) and any other way of staying in touch, such as a 24-hour fax

♦ **Adjust your thinking** Remember that different societies live different lives, have different priorities and different weather and seasonal considerations. For instance, summer in Europe is between June and September (so magazine deadlines are February or April). However, summer submissions for the Australian market carry deadlines of July or August as the holiday months are December to February.

Other matters to consider

When considering the differences it is important not to lose track of the many facets of travel writing that are common to all countries. You will still need to work to a planned schedule, and keep a work log of submissions and deadlines. And you'll still need to deliver meticulously-researched, well-crafted copy that meets the brief – and on time.

If a magazine asks for a foreign-language translation (for example, a bilingual in-flight title), it is important to employ a very sympathetic translator. They will need not only to translate the words but also have a good enough understanding of travel writing to be able keep the meaning, sense and context so that the story works. This is harder than it may seem, because it inevitably means that the article will require extensive re-working – if not a complete rewrite by the translator, which is not an easy or inexpensive task.

Online travel sites are increasingly looking for paid content, offering an outlet for writers keen to add web work to their writing careers. Compared with printed media, the internet attracts fewer competing writers. Online publications tend to be more open to working with new writers and offer budding travel writers a much larger potential audience.

Commissioning is often based on a faster, snappier decision as it works to a shorter editorial lead time in order to keep its content fresh. After years of relying on free posts and material from public travel forums, many of the major online publishers have realised that paid professional content is the only way to get the quality that pulls in the punters. Still, progress is slow in this respect, with unpaid submissions still commonplace. Online markets do not generally pay as well as printed publications – for now, at least. Exceptions include the reputable content providers who contract their work to major commercial clients, such as airlines, cruise liners and credit card companies.

Whoever you establish a writing relationship with abroad it is well worth considering the following points when weighing up its profitability.

♦ Which countries offer the strongest currency? Do I have mechanisms in place to track this to allow me to actively target these sectors during positive fluctuations?

♦ What kinds of features are highly valued by certain foreign markets? Which command the best prices?

♦ Are there opportunities to re-sell articles to multiple publications in different countries to maximise income?

♦ What USPs give me the edge over other writers targeting foreign markets?

♦ Do I have everything in place to enable me to manage deadlines in multiple countries in different time-zones?

SYNDICATION

Certain writing circles can be a bit sniffy about syndicated content. Yet writers who are able to identify topics ripe for syndication are often able to work flat-out all year round. The key to success is versatility as you may be required to cover all manner of topics, from duty-free shopping to malaria, to showbiz holidaying haunts. In essence, syndication involves selling the same article to several publications to get the most revenue from a single piece of work. Many syndication writers sell over 450 stories a year. They are published in magazines and newspapers across the globe – often using pseudonyms.

Almost every travel writer dreams of getting their work published in as many outlets as possible – yet syndication doesn't work in the same way as individual commissioning. Syndication companies sell articles and content to book publishers, newspapers (national, daily and weekly), magazines, society and charity newsletters and websites. They will handle stories and photographs together with cartoons, crosswords, puzzles and brainteasers – basically anything that can be published. Buyers source this content as a cheap way to fill their publications. This is because either they have 'shoestring' staff or because they want their writers to concentrate on other stories, such as hard news or specialist stories. With a syndicate to represent you, it will provide you with more time to focus on the actual writing. You'll still need to promote your services, but you won't need to fill your order book constantly at quite the same pace.

Tips for successful syndication

- Have realistic expectations. You're unlikely to be tackling ground-breaking travel topics so keep an open mind and don't pre-judge.

- Be prepared to really work hard and write every day. A successfully syndicated content writer needs to be prepared to be a prolific writing machine.

- Prove your diligence, reliability and flexibility to ensure you get a reputation for writing well – and to the brief.

- Learn to think like a syndicator. Stories written for the syndication market are usually only semi-topical as they need to have an extended shelf life.

- Be prepared to shift your stance when it comes to payments. With syndication, the pay is low – but if you're a workhorse, you can maximise revenues by securing regular work.

Given the reach of syndication, your articles will almost certainly benefit from widespread distribution into markets that may have been hard to penetrate on your own. The downside of syndication is that writers are paid a fraction of the usual going rate. While greater exposure ought to mean greater financial returns, all too often that isn't how it works out. Most syndication deals involve a 50–50 split of the gross fee. Some companies demand all rights in all media – traditional and electronic – are handed over so that no payment or permission is needed however many times a piece is reproduced. However, as the copyright owner, you should make clear it that you are granting a licence for a particular use only and, if the piece or photograph is to be used again, another fee must be negotiated. The easiest way to do this is to write or email your terms before you deliver the work, so you are covered in case a dispute should arise.

Although some publishers will syndicate on your behalf, another route is to find an independent agency who may give you a better deal. You should also assert your moral right to be credited as the author. Usually, travel pieces should have accompanying pictures supplied as a part of the package, so the publisher has as little work to do as possible. The pictures, though, must be high quality (so around 1MB in size and over 300dpi).

Articles are often run without a full credit. However, syndicate deals vary so it pays to keep an open mind. Start by pitching the larger syndicates that handle submissions from outside writers. You'll find details of companies that handle syndicated travel content by doing a simple search on the internet. Many are self-syndicators that offer limited opportunities for freelancers. However, some companies represent a decent-sized bank of freelance writers and will always want to consider others with prolific skills. Identify the major syndicates open to outside submissions and establish what types of columns and travel topics they sell.

Pitching a syndicate requires a writer to galvanise their 'trumpet blowing' skills. Outline all the credentials and personal attributes that equip you perfectly for syndication (consult your USPs). If you've got a suitable article that sends out just the right message (flexibility, saleability and, of course, great writing) then attach it to your introductory email. It is also a good idea to send a hard copy by post. Be sure to direct the syndication to your website and to mention any awards or merits you've gained to add extra oomph.

Typical articles bought by syndication companies are 950–1,300 word destination features with sidebars on recommended hotels and restaurants and other pertinent information – plus half a dozen photographs. Travel columns are also marketable if the writer is known, acclaimed or a specialist. These normally run to 500–650 words and take a specific hot-topic or seasonal theme. You may be able to find out more about writing syndicated content through a creative writing course, networking activities or association membership. For example, the British Guild of Travel Writers has held highly informative evening talks in the past with key speakers from the industry. Syndication can be a thorny issue and learning the ins and outs first-hand can be invaluable if you are keen to explore the possibilities.

NEW CHALLENGES

Once a travel writer has secured a few commissions, gained confidence and established a comfortable style (or styles), the next step in maximising income is to evaluate ways in which their craft can applied to other – and more lucrative – outlets. Every writer has a distinctive voice and there are many ways in which the compelling material they have gathered can be used. As observers and meticulous researchers, good travel writers often amass considerable knowledge about a specific location and geographical region. Or they may develop an area of expertise such as the Suez Canal, ancient Mayan civilisations, family vacations or the Welsh-speaking population of Argentina.

Some of the most successful travel writers are those who look outside the written form to explore the possibilities beyond magazine features, newspaper articles, web content and guidebooks. They assess the material they have to hand and begin to think laterally about where and how this can be utilised within other commercial areas. As new potential markets emerge, this breed of writer will evolve in style and character to capture the opportunities that these added streams of income bring. Growth in market terms is continual, so travel writers should grow too. As our understanding of the world deepens – and how we interpret it – it is imperative we remain in touch with the demands for our work from other sectors and outlets. With no diploma or publication credit to confer the status of a commercially-savvy travel writer, the ability to turn research material into profit is rarely celebrated or acknowledged. However, dedication to this process is what separates an income-maximising writer from one who can merely write and get published.

Combining the goals of good travel writing and personal development with those of exploring and exploiting all potential money-earning possibilities is what drives incoming-maximising travel writers, be it a toiling author or a feature writer. They devote considerable efforts to self-motivation and marketing within new commercial sectors largely unexplored by travel writers. By setting ambitious benchmarks and evaluating their own worth they are able to take on board the bigger picture in commercial sectors. They no longer feel lucky to have a published portfolio but know they are a resource of significant value. They market their skills and expertise on this basis, certain in the knowledge that there is a buyer for their commodity – the valuable entity that is themselves.

Tour operators

Itinerary development
Every year, hundreds of tour operators add new itineraries to their portfolio of travel options – but these aren't random additions as each has to be accurately evaluated and assessed. Tour operators earn their living from offering travel in an organised and efficient way. They devote considerable time, money and effort into trip planning to ensure the final product will deliver and the holidays they offer are 100% spot on.

Travel itineraries need to balance the expectations, desires, needs and enjoyment of the consumer with making a profit – so transport, accommodation, risks and costs all need to be ascertained with precision. Larger tour operators will often handle multiple destinations so they are rarely experts in each of the countries they sell. As such, they can't possibly have a grasp of the issues that impact on each travel itinerary, such as distances, weather, accessibility and attractions. To develop a prototype they will engage the expertise of others in order to compile, test and refine the product. The expert (or experts) they engage will provide first-hand insight into what is achievable and desirable, from the nitty-gritty of when, what, how and where to specifics such as the nearest hotel to the airport or a great little restaurant stop-off or lesser-known beach. For example, an airport may only be a 7 km drive from the city – but you will know, based on numerous experiences, that in the peak hour melee this is easily a one and a half hour drive. You will also be able to relay the quirks, eccentricities and peculiarities of a place you know inside out, be it the impromptu parties that turn a sleepy village into an all-night rave or the hidden delights of a local food market largely ignored by tourists.

Travel writers can add significant value to a tour operator's itinerary and will often be able to suggest many ways in which a travel option can be unique. In today's ultra-competitive marketplace, tour operators are continually looking for ways to distinguish their business and set it apart from the rest. By employing a trusted resource with a wealth of first-hand knowledge on a particular destination a tour operator can achieve this. You may also be asked to brief a sales team on the destination; to write some copy for the launch brochure; or to deliver a talk on the appeal of the country or resort area to potential customers – each will be a source of revenue.

Author tours

High-end guided tours may also engage travel writers with a speciality to lead their groups as a knowledgeable figurehead. On the basis that 'some tours give you the travel guidebook – but we give you the travel guidebook author' they offer their customers a tangible reason to travel with their company. Using your knowledge of a destination, you'll be called upon to give over-dinner talks each night to highlight what is in store for the following day. Or you may merely be asked to accompany the group, alongside a tour guide, in order to answer questions as they arise along the way.

Cruise companies that specialise in exotic locations often engage travel writers for on-board talks and presentations while adventure tours may call upon an expert for a one-off talk during specific tours.

❛ EARNING PERIPHERAL INCOME

An Expert's View...

I felt that I was extraordinarily lucky to contact an American tour operator specialising in South America the year they set up their business. They needed leaders and I needed a way of continuing to travel in South America. They were quite candid: leaders who had written guidebooks looked good in the brochure. I worked for Wilderness Travel for 15 years in addition to several other UK-based tour operators.

Tour leading gave me much of my material for lectures, which I have given in five different countries, and which provide a regular source of income. I have also lectured on cruise ships, both expedition ships, which combine tour leading and lecturing, and luxury cruise ships.

Once you get a foot in the door, the opportunities keep coming. The trick is not to ask for much money for your first few lectures. Get your hand in with the WI, join the Globetrotters and offer to do a talk, and generally make yourself available. Oh, and you do need to be a good public speaker! ❜

Specialising in unusual destinations and wildlife guides, Hilary Bradt co-founded Bradt Travel Guides in1974. In 2007, she stepped down as MD to concentrate on writing and lecturing and the promotion of responsible travel, focusing on ways of 'giving something back' to local communities. In 2008, she was awarded an MBE for services to tourism and charity. (Visit: www.hilarybradt.com)

Project management

Project management can encompass all manner of activities and responsibilities but travel writers are often employed to develop aspects of a tour company's strategic planning. This could involve producing feasibility reports that pull together tourism research and economic data. Or it could be that you highlight upcoming political or social events that could impact on development decisions.

A travel writer's contacts on the ground are also often worth their weight in gold to a tour company keen to expand in a certain location. You may be able to offer your one-off photographs for use in their marketing materials (brochure, website and posters) or downloadable podcasts for the website. Most tour companies launch their new itineraries with an event that gives a flavour of the destination. Travel writers are often able to provide consultancy in this respect, sourcing music, food, drinks and costumes that provide a true and authentic flavour of the place. Authors who have written books about the destination will be able to sign books and promote sales during such events.

Hotel chains

Globalisation has placed a greater emphasis on the need for cross-cultural training and few environments are as multicultural in makeup as international hotels. As workplaces, hotels often recruit employees from different cultural backgrounds. As properties, they are equally as diverse in the nationalities they attract. Hotels are increasingly aware that they need to continually improve their cross-cultural communications to keep up with the changing demographics of their staff and guests. For example, it wasn't long ago that Eastern European or Chinese hotel guests were a rarity. Today, as borders open and the world becomes more accessible, every hotel around the world needs to understand the contrasting and diverse cultural character of its guests.

Many of the larger international hotel chains offer an inter-cultural training programme especially for hotel operations, to enhance the quality of international service, retain current customers and attract more international customers. Travel writers who have travelled and worked extensively overseas can play an important role in inter-cultural training programmes. Most are keen observers of the individual habits and cultural requirements of the world's many different nationalities – and can convey, without stereotyping, why it is of paramount importance not to assume a 'one size fits all' approach to hotel guests. Some use humour and relate first-hand experience to prepare hotel staff for the surprises and confusion that can arise in complex cultural situations. In some Asian cultures, for example, eye contact is not sought, as it can make guests feel uncomfortable, while in Western tradition it is equated with openness and honesty. Understanding these differences could be important in defining how hotel staff address certain Asian guests.

Generalisations are also useful when used to convey what information check-in staff may need to relay to each guest. For example, it may be typecasting, but an American will generally need to know where he can eat dinner, while an Australian is more likely to want to know where he can find the bar. An English guest is unlikely to complain about a standard-sized double, whereas an American will expect a king-size bed. Knowing where to find a good sushi bar or steak house will please a Japanese guest, while mentioning that the hotel restaurant has a particularly fine wine cellar is likely to be well received by the French. Similarly, having a few words of Arabic up your sleeve will extend a warm welcome to a family from Saudi Arabia, while providing a room with both bath and shower facilities to Japanese guests will show you acknowledge that they favour both in their regime of personal hygiene.

Travel writers can demonstrate that, while it is important not to fall into the trap of stereotyping groups from different cultures, it is crucial to look at the basics that cultural diversity might require of a hotel. Used in conjunction with other workshops and training, the insight of a travel writer can help employees feel comfortable in problematic cultural situations and gain the necessary problem-solving skills. Training agencies run a wide variety of coaching programmes that focus on major national cultures or that target specific cultures or countries. Well-travelled writers with in-depth knowledge of a specific nation or culture can add considerable value to these courses, either by simple lectures, case studies or talks using personal anecdotes of how verbal and non-verbal communication can create a rapport with different cultures and avoid potentially offensive faux pas.

Consultancy

Another area of hotel consultancy for travel writers to consider is new development. Smaller hotels, keen to expand into destinations offering commercial potential, will look to experts to provide reports, statistics and 'investment drivers' (such as political, social or large-scale events) that could impact on planning decisions and timing.

Travel writers are also often called upon to provide feedback during the soft-opening phase of new hotels and should take advantage of paid feedback and critique. One particular travel writer from the UK has made these types of report a trademark of her service. She began by submitting them free-of-charge after every stay and took the time to construct a thoroughly professional detailed summary that comprised extensive feedback on all aspects of the hotel operation from her perspective. Before long, the reports were sufficiently well received for their content that she was able to charge around £500–£750 a piece – and her ideas are now incorporated in hotels all over the world.

However, travel writers who explore this avenue will need to appreciate the need for balance and perspective as there is very little value in a critical onslaught. You'll need to take a broader view, drawing on your experiences of hotels across the world. Bringing the far corners of the world together is part and parcel of what the hotel sector does, so the greatest value is placed on unbiased advisory reports that blend observations (such as which amenities cater for the needs of the world's different cultures) with acknowledgements (such as how you felt the choose-a-pillow-scheme worked or why a women-only floor is particularly worthy of greater promotion) and critique (how things could be done better or the need to add additional features).

These points are core to the success of large, international hotel chains keen to pay closer attention to the trends of globalisation – and most will be prepared to listen to a well-travelled expert to stay ahead of the competition on all aspects of amenities and service.

Tourist boards

Many tourist boards are run by a 'shoestring' permanent staff and so call on outside agencies and expertise to work on ad hoc projects. These projects provide considerable opportunities for travel writers with specialist knowledge in the form of consultancy and promotional campaigns. Many tourist board projects are run by PR agencies appointed to represent their interests and provide a media interface. However, some are handled entirely by in-house employees who often are stretched to capacity and grateful for outside help. Each and every tourist board has a different market focus and way of working with budgets that reflect the importance of the local travel sector.

Travel writers can often get involved with copywriting promotional material (brochures, websites and press releases) and may also be asked to lead specific projects, such as gathering research and developing ideas on how to celebrate a bicentenary or an Olympic bid. With many tourist boards throwing much of their budget into online marketing there is an on-going need for podcasts, on-stream video and interactive FAQs from knowledgeable experts. Tourist boards also run organised press trips for travel writers and journalists and sometimes engage travel writers who know the region well to lead the group alongside a PR representative.

It pays to study the activities of the tourist boards in your specialist destination in order to pitch ideas that highlight your value to their future plans. Many tourist boards organise press events, talks and product launches to coincide with special events and travel trade and consumer shows and exhibitions. The biggest, World Travel Market (WTM) in London each November, is a major date in the calendar and involves mammoth advance planning – so if you're keen to be involved in some way be sure to make contact with the tourist board well in advance.

❛FORGING AHEAD

An Expert's View...

When Proexport Colombia first opened a tourism division in their London office in 2006, it understood the importance of changing perceptions. We needed to encourage travellers to discover Colombia first-hand as a new, exciting destination. We also wanted to convey an important message – that Colombia is very much open to tourists. Travel writers, journalists and authors played a vital role in getting that message across. In the last four years, the Colombian Tourist Board has worked extensively with the travel media worldwide and has invited over 200 journalists, writers and authors to experience Colombia for themselves. We relish the opportunity to work in collaboration with the media as we are confident Colombia offers them a myriad of exciting story angles.❜

Juan Guillermo Perez is the director of Proexport London, the government agency in charge of promoting tourism, trade and investment in the UK. (For more information on Colombia, visit www.colombia.travel)

TV and film production companies

So much of what we watch on television or listen to on the radio involves travel and knowing a location well. Whether they are property TV shows or reality telly, wildlife documentaries or radio outside broadcasts – each requires an element of consultancy, from when to film to avoid the rainy season and find that elusive golden frog, to where to capture that interview against a magical backdrop of a sunset and an idyllic palm-scattered beach.

Travel writers are invaluable to TV and film production companies who need a local insight and insider tips in order to find what they need quickly. In-house location scouts and researchers can't be an expert on every country or region so they will often call upon a writer who knows a place inside out. Some will ask for a full report in synergy with an outline of the production schedule. This will often specify the style of location they need for a particular shot or piece to camera (such as snow-capped mountain or Gothic cathedral) but could also ask you for interview contacts (such as local people with specific experiences or insight) as well as requesting your ideas.

Small independent film-makers and TV producers may also ask travel writers for material in order to lead content, finalise scripts and add in voice-over dialogue. This could take the form of a bullet-point list of key facts for inclusion or it may be a more substantial report. In, say, a travel show, this could include the population of a place, tourist figures, the number of sunny days per year and how many airlines fly there, together with a zillion quirky and engaging topics that may be used to provide the audience with an overview of a location's background, history and current appeal. In the normal course of things, you'll almost certainly be asked to write a set of briefing notes for the production team that details the weather, risks and likely challenges of the destination. In some instances, a travel writer can become a part of the filming process and is asked either to appear on camera, or to tag along on location in an advisory consultancy role.

PR and advertising agencies
Numerous travel industry businesses engage a PR and advertising agency to handle their promotion and publicity. This can take

many forms, from TV commercials and website design, to press liaison, marketing materials (such as brochures, billboards and magazine advertising), to exhibitions and shows.

Travel writers are frequently engaged as a natural extension to the PR and ad agency's operations as the ebb and flow of work dictates. The work varies dramatically, depending on the PR or ad agency and the clients and budgets they handle and represent. However, normally it will span corporate writing, press releases, copy writing and research – so long as there is no conflict of interest. Special events can also include project management and editing, for example in the event of a commemorative book being produced or an in-house newsletter or seasonal supplement.

Generally speaking, PR and advertising agencies operate in a fast-moving world where projects need to be delivered to an exacting brief, to budget and on time. Clued-up, commercially savvy, flexible travel writers can often excel in this area because they can produce high quality copywriting, consultancy and editing services at speed in this time-critical environment.

Other commercial sectors

Healthy tourism and upcoming tourism trends have an impact on many other seemingly unrelated businesses, such as real estate, financial services and the health sector. As a result, many commercial entities commission destination-specific tourism reports on which to gauge their own business strategies. Reports detail in considerable depth the economic, social and political status of a tourism region together with the potential risks and investment drivers that could impact on future growth.

A report writer with an understanding of travel and tourism will need to gather research and statistics from a number of solid, credible, identifiable sources in order to specify travel and consumption, investment (state and private) and measure foreign trade in travel and tourism.

The report should also cover spending on travel (usually split into consumer and business sectors) whilst looking at the supply side of the travel and tourism economy. Other angles may involve studying the environmental impact of travel and tourism or the resulting or upcoming predicted rise in property values due to increased visitor figures in a specific location.

Writing reports

Report writing is different from writing essays or features. It requires a very different discipline although this may vary dramatically from one report to another. Expectations can also be different from one report to the next, even within the same travel and tourism discipline. So it is important to approach every report as an individual project. Consider what the purpose of the report is and who you are writing for, together with the kind of research that you will need to gather. However, the following checklist applies to every type of report format.

- The structure is formal.
- It is informative and fact-based.
- It is written with a specific purpose and reader in mind.
- It is written in a style appropriate to each section.
- Section headings are always included.
- Bullet points are used to list specific key elements.
- Tables and/or graphs are often included.
- Recommendations for action are included.

Poor reports are usually poor because of a failure by the writer to understand the purpose of the report. Common problems could be:

- a failure to meet the brief;
- the report is badly structured;
- an inappropriate writing style has been used;
- it contains poor grammar and punctuation;
- there is incorrect or inadequate referencing;
- there is too much/too little/irrelevant material;
- the expression is not clear;
- the results don't relate to the purpose;
- there is unnecessary use of jargon.

If all this sounds a world away from travel writing then it may help to focus on the similarities. For example, a report is still an act of communication between you and your reader – and just like engaging feature copy it should pay special attention to who the projected reader is and what they want.

Think about why the report is required and make sure you respond to that. Take time to communicate the processes and results of your research clearly and accurately, presenting your findings in the context of the overall purpose. Don't over-complicate your writing; keep your expression clear and simple so that it informs and achieves its purpose rather than muddling the reader with phrases and jargon. Use accurate data and information in non-ambiguous terms and ensure every idea, diagram and piece of information comes from a credible source (such as the World Tourism Council, EU or UN) which must be acknowledged with a reference.

Features of a report

A key feature of a report is the formal structure of sections that have their own purpose and which need to be written in a style to suit that purpose. Understanding the function of each section will help you to structure your information and use the correct writing style. Every report will require different sections, so always check instructions carefully to ascertain exactly what is needed.

Title: This should concisely state the topic of the report, including the particular aspect you are covering and the larger context in which it is situated. Avoid including too much detail in your title – on the other hand, don't make it too general.

Executive summary: This is the 'shop window' for your report. It is the first (and sometimes the only) section to be read and should be the last to be written. It should draw the reader in and allow them to make an informed decision about whether they want to read the whole report. The length will depend on the extent of the work reported, but it is usually a paragraph or two and always less than a page – usually including the answers to the following:

◆ What is the purpose of the work?
◆ What methods did you use for your research?
◆ What were the main findings and conclusions reached as a result of your research?
◆ Did your work lead you to make any recommendations for future actions?

Background: This section allows the writer to explain the rationale for undertaking the work reported on. It should be written in an explanatory style and should state what the report is about – and the question you are trying to answer. If it is a brief for a specific reader (e.g. a feasibility report on a tourism construction project), say who they are. Describe your starting point and the background to the subject, for instance: what research has already been done (if you have been asked to include a Forecast Survey later in the report, you only need a brief outline of previous research in this section); what are the relevant themes and issues; why are you being asked to investigate it now?

Explain how you are going to go about responding to the brief. If you are going to test a hypothesis in your research, include this at the end of your introduction. Include a brief outline of your method of enquiry. State the limits of your research and reasons for them, for example: 'Research will focus on the South American region only, as a proper consideration of the issues arising in other geographic areas is beyond the scope of this project'.

Methodology: In this section, you should outline your approach so that, in theory, the reader could replicate the research you have done. Write clearly with no ambiguity in a very factual informative style. State clearly how you carried out your investigation. Explain why you chose this particular method (questionnaires, focus group, experimental procedure, etc.), include techniques and any equipment you used. If there were participants in your research, who were they? How many? How were they selected? Be thorough and take the reader through what you did step by step, including everything that is relevant.

Findings: This section has only one job: to present the findings of your research as simply and clearly as possible. Use the format that will achieve this most effectively: e.g. text, graphs, tables or diagrams. Think about how the data will look to the reader and choose just one format. Don't repeat the information. Label graphs and tables clearly.

Discussion: As the meat of the report, this section should have adequate time invested in it as it will bring everything together. As the longest part of the report, it should show how your findings respond to the brief you explained in your introduction. Write it in a discursive style.

Conclusions: This short, concise section shouldn't raise new arguments or introduce new evidence – it is a summary of the main points of your research in relation to the original brief. Use this section to specify recommendations for action.

References: Any works you have referred to in the report should be listed in this section, including books, journals, websites and other materials.

Appendices: Use this section to include additional information that may help the reader but is not essential to the report's main findings: anything that 'adds value'. That might include a glossary of terms used. Label all appendices and refer to them where appropriate in the main text (e.g. 'See Appendix A').

Planning your time and work
Plan your time and your work meticulously using the word count and submission date to calculate the scope of the report. For example, a 50,000-word travel and tourism report on the Caribbean region will be expected to include a lot more

background and discussion than a 2,000-word report on a Bedfordshire agro-tourism venture. Allocate sufficient time to write up your work properly, allowing an adequate proportion of this for research (which will often take up 50%). Aim to have a first draft ready several days before the deadline as you will inevitably have to rewrite sections to improve clarity – a vital part of successful report writing.

Generally, it is unlikely that you will be credited as the author of a report if you are commissioned by a commercial entity (such as a bank or property investment company) or agency. However, tourist boards are likely to accredit the report to a specific named author – especially if you are a trusted name in travel writing because it will lend additional credence to the report.

BUILDING ON THE BASICS

Once you've managed to carve out a decent fledgling career in travel writing there is a real temptation to take your foot off the pedal. After all, it has been a hard slog crafting and developing a writing style not to mention all that sales effort to get published and maximise the results. Yet there is arguably no better time to increase effort than when you are enjoying a run of early success. You may be tired of knocking on doors and networking in order to seek out all commissioning possibilities – but with some added oomph it is prudent for travel writers to build on the basics.

In writing terms, the basics may be a steady stream of commissions or a good relationship with a travel publisher keen to sign you up for guidebook work. You've probably got a decent website that serves its purpose and your marketing activities are ticking along nicely with a good rate of pitch-to-sale conversion.

However, now is the time to seize the potential in order to build on more from this level of success – it is no time to rest on your laurels. Take time to re-evaluate your business, to assess your strengths, USPs, mission statement, vision statement and ultimate goals. Be honest, and ask yourself: is there more I could be doing? In 99% of cases, the answer will be a resounding 'yes'.

‘ **CURB THAT COMPLACENCY**

An Expert's View . . .

With a decent portfolio of clients and regular working rhythm, it is easy to let complacency set in. I set aside time at regular intervals to undertake a 'complacency check' – and it never fails to amaze me how much I've let things slip. I can get totally caught up in my writing and when you're busy it's all too easy to miss out on what's going on. A regular review forces me to pull myself back into a more proactive mode. It makes me face up to the need to sell my skills and write concurrently. Also to continue to look at new and alternative revenue streams – a must for money-making travel writers. For me, this 'shake up' is a vital investment in time to keep me right on track. Otherwise, I could easily lose myself in a project only to come up for air having missed a zillion opportunities that passed me by. ’

Sarah Woods (www.sarahwoods.co.uk)

SO, WHAT NEXT?

If you're an author with a published travel narrative or guidebook, then consider the following next steps:

◆ Meet the PR department or publicity agency of the publisher to discuss ways in which you can raise the profile of the book – and the author. Prepare some ideas or, at the very least, arrive armed with bags of enthusiasm and commitment so that you convince everyone concerned that you are worthy of a concerted push. Consider offering yourself as a public speaker in book shops, travel societies, travel exhibitions and travel stores or raise the possibility of book-signings – these are events that you can arrange yourself but it will be easier to enlist the help of paid professionals with a vested interest. After all, if you sell more books or create a buzz, they profit too.

◆ Book sales are largely reliant on big name distributors and online sales, so investigate ways in which you can give them a boost. Every single sale counts – so don't be daunted by the scale of this project. Simply tackle each possibility in a methodical and explorative way and see where it takes you. Amazon rankings can impact on sales, so ensure every reader who contacts you with positive feedback is encouraged to post a review online. Ask them if you can use comments in future marketing campaigns – especially if the feedback is glowing. Reader reviews are invaluable, so be sure to copy them to your publisher. You can also incorporate them in your sales efforts (using 'pull quotes' to maximise their punch) and add them to your website. Make a list of all the websites that you may be able to link to yours to maximise traffic, such as publishers, tourist boards and travel websites. You may be able to generate book sales by adding an e-commerce function to your website linking it to tour operators that specialise in that destination. Ask your publisher for a discounted price to buy a stock of your book and approach all potential sales outlets (tour operators, tourist boards, consulates and embassies) with a special deal on signed copies. This is especially worthwhile ahead of a second edition as it is a good way to shift old stock and ingratiate yourself with the publisher to boot.

- ◆ Launch your own PR offensive to publicise your recent success or trips by contacting local and regional TV, radio and newspapers. Get some postcards printed with the cover sleeve of your book (ask your publisher for a high-resolution digital jpeg image) – for a £20 investment you'll have an impressive looking mailshot. Remember to let friends, family and colleagues know about your book – you'll be surprised how many people will want to snap up a copy.

- ◆ Remember to register your book details on the Public Lending Rights (PLR) website – there are different registrations for the UK and the Republic of Ireland, so be sure to list it twice. PLR is the right for authors to receive payment under PLR legislation for the loans of their books by public libraries. Payments are made annually on the basis of loans data collected from a sample of public libraries in the UK. PLR is funded by the Department for Culture, Media and Sport and receives around £7.5 million of which £6.6 million is distributed to authors. Every single library loan is a potential source of income – so PLR registration is essential for authors. Over 23,000 writers, illustrators, photographers, translators and editors who have contributed to books lent out by public libraries receive PLR payments each year.

- ◆ To qualify for PLR in a book you should be named on its title page or be entitled to a royalty payment from the publisher (but you do *not* have to own the copyright). When two or more contributors are involved they must divide the PLR between them. This is done on the basis of percentage shares which they must agree before applying for registration. Every contributor named on the title page of a book needs to be consulted when agreeing percentage shares and the agreed division should reflect contribution. Each eligible contributor may then submit a separate application, with the following taken into account:

– **writers** – share to reflect contribution;
– **illustrators/photographers** – share to reflect contribution even if paid by fee;
– **translators** – share fixed at 30%;
– **original author** – even if out of copyright or deceased a notional share should be allocated to reflect contribution;
– **adaptors/re-tellers** – 80% of the *text* share (after the illustrator's share is allocated) where the original author is named on the title page *or* 100% of the *text* share where no original author is named;
– **ghost writers** – if named on the title page *or* entitled to royalties from the publisher;
– **editors/compilers/abridgers/revisers** – share to reflect contribution.

◆ Where a contributor has died or cannot be located, the remaining contributor(s) may still register a share. If similar books have been registered in the past, the same share agreement may stand. If not, the shares should be reasonable in relation to the actual contribution. Before submitting your application you must take into account all eligible contributors named on the title page (refer to the information above), and apply to register a share which reflects your individual contribution to the book(s). Authors can apply online or download an application form from: www.plr.uk.com.

FEATURE WRITERS AND AUTHORS

If you've got what appears to be a nice, steady flow of work from a particular editor it is important not to take this for granted. Reiterate how much you are enjoying the working relationship and explore ways in which you may be able to build on it – you may be able to turn monthly commissions into an annual retainer or a more profitable role, such as features editor. If your commissioning editor is happy with you, the chances are they will welcome your suggestions with a view to trying incorporating them, in whole or in part, in future plans.

Feature writers with a talent for good descriptive colour pieces are often able to use their skills in other genres. Consider branching out to add travel poetry or children's literature on a travel theme to your publishing credits. Always dreamt of writing a script? Then start playing around with ideas for a travel-based sitcom, drama or movie – the process is surprisingly easy for writers used to the discipline of structured writing. Several UK travel writers also write radio plays. Others are published lyricists with a number of TV dramas under their belts.

Another option to explore is creative writing mentoring or tutoring at the many courses and workshops run in colleges, schools, universities and private enterprises across the UK and the world. Numerous establishments across the globe welcome visiting writers into their ranks for specialist presentations as do community-based initiatives, summer schools and journalist training programmes. Pen an introductory letter outlining your credentials and experience to the head of English or creative writing. The Open University also recruits creative writing mentors on an annual basis.

Register as an expert in travel at one of the many online resource specialists. You can use a myriad associated words to ensure you come up in all relevant searches. Major broadcasters rely on these banks of experts for their TV news, radio, web TV and film productions. In many instances a daily fee is paid with expenses covered at the very least – but this is a great way to increase your profile from just a writer into a knowledgeable authority.

❛ SPECIALISTS ARE EXTRA-SPECIAL

An Expert's View...

Working with contributors who really know their subject is immensely rewarding. Many of our contributors started out as generalists who developed specialist knowledge of the Caribbean. Others have always worked in niche markets. Being an authority on a specific place or destination can be a huge advantage, as a writer is often best placed to offer unique, inside stories and news pieces because they have their ear to the ground. They can become an authority on the subject, which can lead to all sorts of spin-off activities. This not only strengthens their writing in many instances, but can also make them a prized commodity. Every magazine wants the best and most knowledgeable writers for their commissions – *and* Caribbean World *is no exception.* ❜

London-based Ray Carmen is the publisher of *Caribbean World* magazine, a glossy consumer title that covers all things Caribbean, from lifestyle to real estate, published quarterly with spring, summer, autumn and winter issues.
(Visit: www.caribbeanworld-magazine.com)

$$\left(6\right)$$

Developing Your Business

> ❛ *I soon realised that no journey carries one far unless, as it extends into the world around us, it goes an equal distance into the world within.* ❜

Lillian Smith

BOOSTING RESILIENCE

Travel writers who yearned to work for themselves may have felt daunted at the prospect of running a small business. Yet, they pushed ahead on the basis of freedom and independence and made it work. Then, just as things are ticking along nicely, they realise they have to face a new set of dilemmas – balancing the demands of being the business as a sole trader and the vulnerability that brings. Consider the following major risks:

- sudden illness or unforeseen periods of absence;
- computer systems and viral attack;
- copyright, legal issues and indemnity insurance;
- plagiarism, internet piracy and scams;
- banking terms and arrangements;
- bad debt and cashflow;
- reliance on a single customer or small client base.

Illness and unforeseen absence

Every small business is vulnerable because of its size and reliance on the founder – and travel writers are no exception. What happens if you are off for a couple of days or need to take time off work for a family emergency? Most travel writers will admit they have no kind of backup plan. After all, it is not as if you can employ a temp to cover in your absence. No, in most cases, an illness or time away from work means that the business effectively grinds to a shuddering halt. Because unless they are lucky enough to employ an assistant or to work with other freelancers as a team – for most travel writers they *are* the business. While a few days off with a stomach bug may be inconvenient and disruptive, a broken arm or sustained illness could cause considerable devastation to your business and your finances. So it may pay to plan ahead for this situation as a contingency – just in case you are waylaid by a medical mishap or prolonged absence from work.

❛FREELANCING IN AN UNCERTAIN ECONOMY? SIMPLE: BE CREATIVE

An Expert's View...

When commissions start dropping off, start thinking of new angles and publications for your stories. Everyone wants to write for the biggies, but the reality is that many other magazines and rags pay better, commission more regularly and are easier to deal with. Not every commission you seek needs to be from Condé Nast Traveller. *Why shouldn't you write about tooling around Oxford on a bike for* Velo News? *Or* Oxfordshire Life? *Or the* South China Morning Post? *Also, don't be afraid to be assertive with editors when it comes to chasing pitches. As publisher William Feather succinctly put it, "Success seems to be largely a matter of hanging on after others*

have let go." And remember: Be Nice To Everyone. It's honey over
vinegar in the freelance world, and you never know when today's
mailroom boy will become tomorrow's editor-at-large.
⟩

Roger Norum (www.norums.com) is an award-winning travel journalist and
guidebook author. He has written for the *Guardian*, the *Independent* and
Departures and a number of inflight magazines, and he has co-authored Rough
Guides to Denmark, Finland and Scandinavia. Roger teaches regular travel
writing retreats and workshops with Creative Escapes.
(Visit: www.creative-escapes.co.uk)

Having a business contingency strategy should be an early priority
– but in reality it rarely is. However, when travel writers begin to
develop their business it should become a part of boosting its
resilience with regular reviews as the business evolves. Start by
creating a list of all the critical and non-critical processes and
procedures that are necessary to run your business. Prioritise them
in order of importance and detail what each involves – and why
and when. Make sure you include the little idiosyncrasies that are
unique to your style of business management. Detail any special
relationships you have with certain editors, publishers or suppliers
and ensure your sales diary and upcoming commission records are
fully up to date. This means that at a push, someone else could
step in to firefight should you be delayed for a month in a war-
torn nation. It will also help to protect your income if you are
unlucky enough to be holed up in airport for over a week thanks
to an industrial dispute or hurricane.

Often, by itemising your daily routine and having all the basics
written down as a process, many freelancers feel comforted by the
fact that they have the business mapped out. It can offer some
peace of mind to know that someone could feasibly chase up

outstanding monies on your behalf. It can also bring a great sense of relief to travel writers to know that a relative or friend could step in to contact clients and suppliers. It is better if they have a sensible explanation for your absence than to wonder why you've simply disappeared off the radar.

Almost three in five (59%) of UK businesses would not survive if a key player were lost from business with well over two thirds (83%) reliant on one key person. Some 62% of small businesses fail to insure this key player, with 90% of sole traders not doing enough to protect themselves from the unexpected, such as illness. Worse still, around 11% haven't even considered how vulnerable they are. In simple terms, modern medical science means that you will probably survive a heart attack – yet evidence suggests your business may die a death while you're regaining full health.

Computer systems and viral attacks

Another area of vulnerability is computer hackers who, according to systems gurus, consider small business targets easy prey. By adopting the 'it won't happen to me' approach (almost certainly based on a false sense of security that they don't have anything worth hacking into) sole traders – including travel writers – are particularly at risk. Small business owners rarely invest in information technology security or if they do, integrate only minimal security measures, leaving them open to an outside attack.

Yet hackers attack every 39 seconds, so no business can consider themselves invincible – especially if they only have a spam filter and standard virus check. Unlike most sole traders or freelancing travel writers, hackers use the latest in sophisticated technology.

They can watch you type in real-time, turn on your webcam and/ or microphone, access your passwords, turn off your virus protection and shut down your desktop – so heightened security is paramount whatever size your business operation. Indeed, given the amount of web-based research and sustained periods online, travel writers are particularly prone to hacker penetration. However, by implementing some simple, low-cost business-orientated solutions (rather than relying on domestic anti-virus measures more geared to occasional use) you can be better protected. This includes maintaining software and hardware to include upgrades, spyware and antivirus software. Also, make sure your travel laptop has sufficient security protection in case it is stolen or lost. Travel writers also need to invest in high-quality archiving systems to store material and photographs securely and protect them from malware attack.

❛ BETTER TO BE SAFE THAN SORRY

An Expert's View...

As a travel photographer, my many thousands of images are a vital source of income. The one thing I always do without fail every day is take the time to back-up, archive and secure my work. In my mind, my photographs are exactly the same as cash reserves. I wouldn't leave piles of £50 notes scattered around so I make sure I treat my photographs with the same care and attention. Apart from peripherals and camera equipment, my overheads are low as a freelancer. A large percentage of my annual outlay is spent on ensuring I have secure IT that offers me peace of mind. After all, my photographs are the most precious of commodities. I guard my wallet and my credit card against theft and loss – and do exactly the same when it comes to pictures. Of course, like every freelance I have my lazy days when everything seems too much effort. However, to me, taking a lax approach to protecting my photographs from loss and system failure is much the same as leaving an online bank account vulnerable.

Spanish-based Juan Carlos Eleno is a freelance film producer and travel photographer. His photographs have been published all over the world. (E-mail: juancarlos@elviaje.es)

Of course no business can guard 100% against cyber terrorism – even Tibetan spiritual leader the Dalai Lama suffered at the hands of hackers, apparently as the result of a well-designed email lure. However, in recent years a number of travel writers have suffered the devastating viral effect of rogue attacks. Hackers have been able to break into email systems and send messages to publishers and editors who then unwittingly clicked on malicious links in highly plausible communications. Malware was also delivered by stealing legitimate email in transit and replacing attachments with toxic ones – causing widespread data loss.

Copyright, legal issues and indemnity insurance

A number of specialist insurance companies offer policies for writers, journalists and broadcasters often with reduced rates for part-time professionals. With the no-win-no-fee litigious culture bringing indemnity insurance to the fore, this type of cover is well worth considering. It is a complex issue and each travel writer should view their situation as being unique, seeking professional advice accordingly. Indemnity insurance can help in instances where you and your publisher are dragged through the courts on the basis your writing is considered libellous, an invasion of privacy, copyright infringement (or plagiarism), an error and/or omission, product disparagement or harmful to readers (for example, health information). To absolve responsibility for such lawsuits, many publishers include an indemnification clause in their contracts that holds the writer responsible for legal costs if someone sues over their writing content. An increasing number of travel writers who work in foreign markets are taking up indemnity cover on the basis that they want peace of mind, should such a hefty lawsuit come their way.

Scams and internet piracy

Unfortunately, there are numerous crooked practices that target writers and authors – some of them alarmingly successful. In the US in 2009, one shady publishing firm relieved authors all over the world of around $5 million. Yet even though this particular firm was closed down, many more continue to take advantage of authors and writers-to-be. Some scams are sufficiently sophisticated they even fool seasoned writers, often by using replica insignia and familiar publishing jargon to put their targets at ease.

Every scam is different but there are some tell-tale signs that should arouse suspicion. Most are email-based approaches purporting to serve writers in return for a relatively low-level fee. Despite the fact that it doesn't cost the earth, it is important to check the legitimacy and validity of every solicitation. Sniffing out scams before you reveal your credit card number will not only protect your finances but will also save you from being another rip-off statistic. However, be warned, some of these 'publisher approaches' don't ask for money – just for a manuscript or article submission. In every way this is the normal way you may do business, so you're more than happy to meet the brief. In the following days, you're likely to receive an email praising your work. It suggests a literary agency which it is willing to recommend you to by introduction. They tap into the ego of a writer, by pumping it up with false hopes and flattery – taking the time to pinpoint specific phrases or chapters that completely blew them away. So, you submit your work to the literary agency who requests a 'reading fee' as standard (sometimes they refer to it as a contract fee or retainer). It tends to be a manageable amount – nothing extortionate, which is why so many writers don't consider it a scam. After all, 20 bucks or £15.99 is hardly going to break the bank. However, the best agents do not charge reading fees – so consider anyone who ask you for money as greedy, incompetent or disreputable (and probably all three).

Other publishing rip-offs revolve around co-publishing deals that encourage writers to invest which then fail to deliver the goods. Some masquerade as poetry or writing contests offering big prizes for quality submissions – but then also ask for money after showering the writer with praise.

Take the time to check out anything fishy by investigating these questionable literary outfits or post a notice asking writers for their own experiences – the collective wisdom of other writers who experienced the same rip-off is invaluable in this situation.

To avoid being susceptible, scrutinise every approach and ask yourself: 'does it sound too good to be true?' If it does, it probably is.

Another growing problem faced by published authors is internet piracy with the number of complaints made through professional associations all over the world on a steep upward trajectory. Some literary organisations have dedicated extra resources to providing information on how writers can protect copyrighted works. Others are offering practical help on how to fight the growing problem of piracy on the net. As theft of intellectual property affects all creators, the hope is that a combined effort will encourage authors to raise awareness of this issue through direct action.

Campaigners across world are already providing tips on how authors and writers can demand 'take down' of copies of their works. Some American literary websites are already naming and shaming sites that contain unauthorised downloads or other copies of copyrighted novels. The list includes contact information for the website administrators and links to each website's takedown procedures. The Digital Millennium Copyright Act requires online service providers to promptly block access to infringing material (or remove such material from their systems) when they receive notification claiming infringement from a copyright holder. In the UK, writers are encouraged to tackle the issue of internet piracy head on.

Authors and writers are particularly vulnerable to internet piracy and it is important that every freelance travel writer remain aware of where and how their work is being used. To protect your material – and ultimately your source of income – write and complain to the website administrator using the template on page 208.

In October 2008, Google agreed to pay a settlement of $125 million to authors and publishers to resolve a lawsuit led by the US Authors Guild against its Google Book Search initiative. The

[*Date*]

Dear [*site name*] Administrator,

It has come to my attention that my book(s), [*title(s)*] (hereinafter referred to as the 'Copyrighted Work(s)'), has/have been posted [*or made available for download*] on [*site name*]. I located the [*downloadable file(s)*] copy(s) of the Copyrighted Work at the following URL(s) on [*day/month/year*].

URL [*list each violation with sufficient detail for the site administrator to find it*].

As owner of the Copyrighted Work, I request that you promptly remove it from your site as neither I nor any agent of mine gave permission for it to be posted there. I have a good faith belief that there is no legal basis for such use. Pursuant to the **Digital Millennium Copyright Act (in relation to the US)** and **EU Copyright Directive (in relation to the EU)**, I affirm under penalty of perjury that, as owner, I am authorised to request that the Copyrighted Work be taken down. I further affirm that the information in this notification is accurate. [*Check with your publisher to ensure the accuracy of this statement prior to sending any letter*]

I trust that this matter will be dealt with in a timely manner. Contact me using the information listed below once the Copyrighted Work has been removed from [*site name*].

[*Author*]
[*Email address or physical address*]
Sincerely,

[*Author's name*]

settlement enabled authors and publishers to receive compensation for online access to their works as a result of Google's digitising programme in many major American libraries. Representing more than 8,000 authors, the Authors Guild sued Google in 2005, alleging that by digitising works it was guilty of 'massive' copyright infringement. Five large publishers followed the Guild's lead, filing separate lawsuits as representatives of the Association of American Publishers.

Under the terms of the settlement, Google is permitted to make whole pages of copyright works available online. Up to 20% of a book will be accessible for preview, allowing consumers to decide to purchase the book if they so wish.

A free online portal to Google's digitised collection will soon be offered by all American libraries. In 2009 authors and publishers of tens of thousands of out-of-print books submitted claims for compensation from Google Book Search following details of the settlement being published in 218 countries and 72 languages worldwide.

Banking terms and arrangements

If, as a small business, you've not investigated your banking options thoroughly it could end up costing you money. Check that you are still getting a good deal and, just as importantly, good support from your branch. If not, it could benefit your business to switch banks. The money your business spends on banking can add up over the year – all money better off helping your business. You could pay for a business mobile phone, buy new software or even a new PC with the money saved.

Be sure to do your homework to ensure you find the bank that is right for you – but don't stop there, a continual review is an important part of business banking. Shop around to ensure you get the best deal – and check that your bank offers the following.

- No fees – completely free and unlimited.
- Free cash deposits.
- Online account management by telephone or through mobile internet.
- Competitive interest rates.
- Card misuse insurance.
- Travel accident cover.
- Purchase protection.
- Extended warranty.
- Fraud protection.
- Discounts and special deals from other companies.

Over 24% of small firms change their account provider at some stage but is important that having made the switch, your new bank gives you what you need. Consider the branch and helpline opening hours (late evening and weekends), bank charges and fees for using cash cards in the UK and abroad together with online and telephone banking facilities, borrowing facilities, savings options, interest rates and introductory offers. Securing the best rates will go a long way to the smooth running of small business banking transactions. With good quality banking you'll be better placed to calculate figures and projections to ensure your financial goals are realistic and attainable. Reasons to switch your bank account may include:

* fewer bank charges;
* more interest on in-credit balances;
* dissatisfaction with your relationship with your current bank;
* there is no convenient access to your account at the moment.

A staggering 11% of customers in a recent survey said their bank gave poor customer service and 12% rated the service poor due to high charges and/or low interest rates. If we felt this way about our dentist or car mechanic we'd make a switch pronto. This is all about your hard-earned money, so if you're unhappy   move, but be sure to establish that your new bank doesn't have the same failings as the one you ditched.

Bad debt and cashflow

Every year, British businesses write off tens of thousands of pounds in bad debt due to customers not paying their bills. On average, small businesses write off an average of £14,000 in bad debt – a staggering amount when you consider that as a 5% profit margin they would have to drum up additional sales of £280,000 to cover the loss. One in five of all UK firms admit bad debt is now a serious problem with a third of all companies admitting that late payment also has a serious impact. In 2009, the bad debt problem escalated in line with the rising trends in personal and corporate insolvencies. The situation leaves small businesses particularly vulnerable, with the rising trend of bad debt and late payment spurring more sole traders into taking pre-emptive measures to ensure they get paid.

However, for many travel writers, it is difficult to know when a debt turns bad. Dealing with poor payers is a small business nightmare – and it is often tricky to ascertain when a tardy customer becomes a serious payment risk. Prolonged absences and constant travel can present problems for travel writers keen to keep a firm check on their debtor list. However, the nature of the business does not matter – all businesses should expect to be paid, even those run by a roving sole trader. If you haven't set out your stall clearly, then it can be far easier to make the sale than it is to collect the money. It is always important to let clients know your payment terms upfront as you are less likely to run into debt recovery problems as a result.

Most travel writers work to a 30-day rule for payments – but few publishers pay within 60 days. So straight away there is a disparity. Bad debts kill small firms and fast-growing businesses are particularly susceptible, due to investing cash quicker than they can get it in.

A small business should be particularly structured when collecting payments, with simple terms of trade that spell out how and when you expect to be paid. If a project is sufficiently large, it can be worth invoice factoring, whereby the actual debt is sold to an agency for, say, 90% of its value. Otherwise, you should make your own timetable for following up unpaid accounts and make sure you stick to the dates. Set aside some time each week to evaluate the progress of payments, write letters and chase up outstanding monies by phone. Yes, it is an annoyance to have to dedicate time to what should happen automatically (after all, you met your side of the deal by meeting the brief and the deadline – so why can't your client meet theirs?). Yet, if you're prepared to swallow the upfront cost in time and lost income the rewards can be worth it – as a day spent chasing money isn't nearly as expensive as your business suffering because of a cashflow squeeze.

If you're trying to get payment from a small publishing entity, it may mean hassling the very person who commissions you for work. If this is the case, try to take the relationship part of the process out of it by asking someone else to make the call on your behalf. Although you are unlikely to lose business because you are chasing for money, using a third party can save awkwardness on both sides.

If you've sent the reminders, provided the documentation, chased on the phone and are still waiting for payment to materialise there is no avoiding the next step – getting serious and being firm but tough.

Send a collection schedule to your debtor to dictate how you will manage specific amounts of outstanding money over specific amounts of time. For example, £200 overdue by 30 days – a warning letter with threat of legal action; £1,000 overdue by 30 days – passed to collection agency and then chased up by solicitor after another 30 days if the debt is still outstanding.

Consider also detailing the interest charges that will accumulate on overdue bills at X% – a perfectly reasonable and legal option that can be included in your terms of trade. Current legislation allows companies to charge interest on overdue accounts at 8% over and above the Bank of England base rate. Often the threat of extending the debt is enough to prompt immediate payment. However, if this still carries no sway then issue a stern, standard letter from a solicitor. If this fails to generate a swift response you'll then need to consider the Small Claims Court service (at a cost of £80).

Another option for particularly difficult payers is to enlist the help of a collection agency. Many specialist firms collect debts on a 'no collection – no fee' commission basis at a rate of between 5% and 15%, depending on the case. Whatever your approach, it is important not to simply ignore the issue until it is too late. Should the company concerned go under, you'll be unlikely to receive anything – so it is important to strike while the iron is hot to stand a chance of recovering the debt.

Common excuses for late or delayed payment

- **'We haven't received the invoice.'** Send regular statements of account and record when and how you sent it. Address it specifically to the person concerned and fax it with a recorded delivery postal copy addressed to your specific contact.

- **'There are no cheque signatories available.'** Most businesses require two signatures. If the debt is seriously outstanding and only one signatory is available, ask the debtor to authorise their bank to pass the cheque with just one signature – reminding them of your payment terms and conditions.

- **'The cheque is in the post.'** Ah, the time-worn perennial favourite is still alive and well. If the payment does not materialise within two days, ask for the cheque number, the address it was sent to and whether it was sent by first- or second-class post.

- **'The person you need to talk to is in a meeting.'** Ask the debtor to specify when you should call back and then ring at that specific time. Send a fax or email confirming the time you are ringing.

- **'Our computers are down at the moment.'** Establish how long the systems are likely to be down for. Agree a time to call again and fax details of your outstanding payments.

- **'Our terms are XX days.'** There isn't much you can do about this, although if the terms have changed you should insist on knowing when and why. Make a note of the revised terms as outlined by the debtor – and chase it up as soon as the date draws nigh.

- **'We don't have a payment run until next month.'** Insist on an alternative form of payment such as a manual payment cheque. For future reference find out when their cheque runs are.

- **'I am unable to raise manual cheques**.' This is highly unlikely. Rather than unable to, they mean they can't be bothered. Persist in requesting one until they relent.

Reliance on a single customer or a small client base
Huge numbers of small businesses across the UK rely on a single customer for over 75% of turnover – leaving them vulnerable to a sudden change in purchasing or personnel. Most small businesses develop a dependency on a single client because it is championed by a specific customer contact.

Travel writers can often become a favoured contributor to a publishing entity with on-going needs that keep them busy on a week-by-week basis. It is all too easy to accept that the relationship will last without honestly appraising the situation. For example, the magazine could go through management changes and your champion could be redeployed, resign, switch jobs or get fired. In the publishing world, many companies are acquired or acquire other companies resulting in a widespread change in the internal dynamics of your interactions. You are unlikely to receive any warning with the change effected within a matter of days. What you have done for the company before counts for little. A new structure or person is installed and you can only sit and wonder as the weakness from your dependency is fully exposed.

The lesson here for travel writers is that as you line up your first client, you need to redouble your efforts to line up additional customers too. Whatever you do, never rely on a single client for too long – aim for a client base that offers a potential cushion should 50% of your clients disappear overnight. It is better to have six clients who offer you equivalent work than a single client – because you've spread the risk rather than rely on one income stream. Having multiple clients strengthens your position in terms of negotiation and makes you less vulnerable when it comes to bad debt (see page 211).

MANAGING CURRENCY

By managing your portfolio of international publishers it is possible to maximise your currency deals in order to reap the rewards of large increases in value against the pound. For example, writing for a Jamaica-based magazine in June 2009 would have given you 23.97% more than if you'd worked for it in January of the same year. In the same time period the Icelandic krona rose by 22.79% with the Polish zloty up 19.14%. At the other end of the scale you'd have lost 6% of the value if you'd written for a magazine in Brazil and be down by 5.68% in South Africa. Only the Canadian dollar stayed stable with a drop of just 0.5%. In 2009, travel writers would get 12.3% more than the previous year working for a Mauritius-based publisher, 11.8% more in Indonesia but just 3.6% more in Hong Kong.

Foreign exchange rates are one of the most uncertain aspects of travel writing for publications abroad. Even small currency fluctuations can have a serious impact on the profitability of an editorial commission. Exchange rates change every second, meaning that the price you agree with the editor may not be the price you end up with in the bank. So, it is important to negotiate fees in the currency that will give you the best rate of exchange – push for sterling if the pound is your preferred option or stick with the local denomination if that is preferable. Your banking arrangements should offer you a decent deal on premiums charged for currency receipts while your own currency exchange tracking should help to protect you against adverse currency changes.

Travel writers who need to access their cash abroad should be sure to check what their bank charges for the use of a cash card or credit card abroad – Nationwide, for example, don't charge at all.

When spending extended periods abroad in a single-currency zone, be sure to look into a bulk currency buy from foreign exchange specialists. Most guarantee no commission charges, no transfer fee and no international bank receiving costs. Unlike the currency desks at high street banks, foreign exchange specialists allow you to fix a favourable exchange rate for up to a year. Even single money transfers are around 4% lower than the major banks with preferable rates for all online services. As they have lower overheads than the UK's high street banks, foreign exchange specialists can buy in currency cheaper. They make their profit from the difference between their buy and sell prices, i.e. 'the spread' – and so are able to pass their savings on to their customers.

AGENTS AND REPRESENTATION

Literary agents take care of all the tasks involved with helping you to find a publisher. They submit your work to publishers, represent you in negotiations, secure the best publishing deals and resolve any problems between you and the publisher. A very good reason to find yourself a literary agent is that some publishers only accept manuscripts via an agent. They also know all the jargon – like any business publishing has developed its own language. Agents exist to navigate the process for you – and in UK publishing these processes are continually evolving in response to the declining level of book sales.

Just 20 years ago, when a commissioning editor received good material from an agent they'd acquire and instruct the publicity department and the sales team to sell it. Today things have changed. Now an editor will first have to share it with colleagues in the editorial team before attempting to win the support of every other part of the process – marketing, sales and rights. Then they will try to acquire the book. Today it is almost impossible to predict what will sell in bookshops but a proposition needs to carry the hope of making money. This one important factor is a major reason why new authors find it hard to get published – few publishers are prepared to take a risk on an unknown writer and stake their career on what may be a dismal failure.

Finding an agent

To find an agent prepared to take on a new author isn't easy. You'll need to convince them that it is worth their while representing you rather than focusing their efforts on better known authors. It is important to recognise the priorities of an agent so that you can understand how much time will be allocated to you. Many agents simply won't consider new writers. The only way to know who will is to trawl through the trade reference books, visit the agency websites, phone and ask.

There is no sure-fire way to make a successful approach to an agent, but you certainly need to check their stated preferences to make sure you are suitable. Present your work to its best advantage by using a covering letter as an introduction together with a brief synopsis (250–400 words) and the first 10,000 words of your manuscript – it's this sample text that should really do the sales work.

Don't expect a speedy reply; agents can often take weeks and sometimes months to read the manuscript and respond. New material is always at the bottom of daily priorities but if you've had no reply after a month then a follow-up call is the next step. If your manuscript has gone down well, they will request the full script, and this may lead to an offer to represent you. An honest and frank conversation will allow the agent to tell you that there are no guarantees. Plenty of great novels go unpublished, they will stress, and yours could be one of them.

It is likely that your manuscript will require some revisions ahead of being submitted to a publisher – so your agent will discuss how to get it as close as possible to perfection. Often, this is the first time the author will have been exposed to creativity versus commerce – as revision after revision attempts to transform their manuscript into a saleable commodity.

A strong agent will guide the author through the process before taking over entirely to approach the commissioning editors that are the best fit for your book. Using a carefully crafted pitch letter your agent will market your manuscript, often setting a deadline, either for initial responses, or for offers. Every editor who wants to acquire the book will make an opening bid before the agent asks for improved offers. As you lose some bids along the way, a winner will often emerge. Of course, very often no one offers for the book and the manuscript never reaches the offer stage.

Managing the process

Throughout everything you should be able to rely on your agent to manage every process, right up to and beyond publication. At its core, your relationship with them should be a friendship in which both parties trust and respect each other during all the ups and downs. A good agent will demonstrate considerable pride in a client's work and will be there to share in all the joys – and frustrations.

As with all successful relationships, your agent should be your confidante and mentor. If you don't achieve this connection then wait until you meet an agent that you know is right for you. Today, agents recognise that they have to work harder on proposals and manuscripts than ever before in order to seize the best chance of a sale – and the most determined will give it all they've got. So choose wisely and get the partnership right and you'll benefit from an industrious champion – and you'll know that your agent is worth every penny of their 15%.

'A VERY SPECIAL AGENT

An Expert's View...

There is no point in writing a beautifully-crafted travel book if nobody will ever get to read it. Obtaining a publishing deal should give you the promotion you need to hook buyers and the target press. However, in order to secure on-going success it may be necessary to employ a publicist or agent to keep the momentum going.

For an author, searching for an agent or publicist can appear daunting. My advice is to seek someone with whom you feel comfortable. To build a productive relationship, this person will want to know all about you and the inspiration behind your work. On behalf of you and your book they will contact the media. They may also be involved in arranging book launches and promotional events. Ideally you want this to be a lasting relationship so it is important to choose an agent or representative carefully. Meet the person in the flesh and find out who else they are working for. See what makes them tick and assess if they can give you the right amount of time and commitment your work deserves. It's great if you click with your agent as the relationship works best if it is not purely centred on professional representation – but on friendship and loyalty as well.

Stuck for ideas on how to find an agent or representative? Then check out the Writers Hand Book. *Another good source of information is the Society of Authors.*

Jacqui MacCarthy is a seasoned PR professional and Managing Director of d'Image Ltd. She represents a number of acclaimed travel writers and authors and works extensively with travel professionals across the world. (Email: jacqui@d-image.co.uk, tel: 01628 522 982, or visit: www.d-image.co.uk)

Promotional work

Many authors will find that they still need to do some of their own promotion even with a publishing deal and representation. The majority of writers and authors with a publishing deal will be faced with a promotional void that only they can fill. A book is a product and like any other piece of manufactured material it needs selling. The person who knows the product best is the salesperson for the job – that's you, the author.

Promoting a book is a really hard slog and it is crucial to maximise every opportunity. With over 200,000 published every year in the UK alone (and 400 daily in the US), you need to help yours stand out from the crowd. At the centre of promotion is the author, who nowadays has to be prepared to throw themselves into selling their book just as they did into writing it.

Hiring a professional to manage the publicity allows an author to concentrate on that all-important second book. A co-ordinated promotional effort will focus on interviews on TV and radio, press coverage and events staged to give you and your product the highest possible profile. A publicist's main job is media relations, scheduling interviews, book reviews and feature stories for a client. Occasionally, other services are offered, such as book tour co-ordination and promotion, media training and the development of marketing materials. However, a publicist does not typically find agents, publishers or distributors for the book. They may help schedule speaking engagements or coordinate travel arrangements for a book tour – but with the author's help.

Some authors are willing to do just about anything to get their work noticed. Many, however, prefer to stick to a type of promotion that suits their own character and style. As the author is the person doing the selling, the author is in the front line. So, if silly gimmicks aren't your thing state this early on so that you've not wasted anyone's time and energy. Radio interviews can be pre-recorded and presenting talks to libraries and book groups are always rewarding experiences. Of course, nobody expects an author to be an entertaining audience-pleaser – you're a writer not a media personality. Stick to what you do best and allow the book to sell itself. However, as an author, it is important that you make yourself available for promotional activities, be it jumping on train for a TV slot in Scotland or attending a travel show at Earls Court in London. Any promotional specialist will tell that you've got to be prepared to go that extra mile to give a book a real, concerted boost. It's a marathon – not a sprint – so you'll need to put in some sustained energy and effort.

Nowadays, alongside the events and media exposure, a publicist may also use social bookmarks (people-powered search engines) to boost its presence online. When your website is bookmarked and tagged with the topic of your book, other individuals can use these bookmarks for searching when they are looking for a subject. The more a web page is bookmarked, the more popular it becomes, bringing additional traffic to your site and higher search engine rankings.

Printed markcting materials serve as a visual cue every time someone sees them so it may help to have a stock as giveaways for promotional events. Collateral (as printed marketing materials are sometimes called) such as bookmarks, business cards or postcards promoting your book help to remind people that they met you.

Alongside your other publicity activities, they build legitimacy, increase your book's visibility, and serve as a stepping stone for an eventual sale. Even if there isn't a budget for these items, many authors feel it is a valid expense and agree to shell out themselves. A box of 500 bookmarks, for example, will cost around £50 while a similar quantity of postcards will work out at £75.

SELLING THE DREAM

OK, your travel book has made it to the stores and is neatly displayed on the shelves. Your publisher, distributor and sales reps have done their jobs – now it's time to do yours. Over 75% of books fail to earn back their advance. Over 50% of all books are returned, remaindered, or destroyed without a page being turned. Authors keen to do something to improve their sales should consider working with a promotional specialist or representation. The following activities can all be easily author led and run in conjunction with your publisher's (or your representative's) own PR campaign efforts.

Autographed books sell better than their unsigned counterparts. So explore ways in which you can offer signed books as a value-added purchase. A good first step is to list all the stores within easy reach of your home in, say, a 60-mile radius. Independent booksellers are generally happier to see you, and more eager to sell your books. Contact as many as possible, along with a mix of big-name stores. Make time for, say, a three-day signing and offer each book outlet an option of two days and times. Try to avoid the overly-structured process favoured by the large book retailers and deal with the branch manager direct.

Once you have your scheduled confirmed, send it to your agent and publisher. The fact that you have organised it will demonstrate your commitment to publicity and promotion. Not only will it impress them but it will also give them something to take to the press. Check that the store is ordering sufficient stock for you to sign – or that it already has enough on the shelves. In reality, you're unlikely to cause a stampede with a travel narrative or guidebook – but you also don't want to drive 60 miles to scribble your name on a single copy.

In advance of the book signing, get a good stack of postcards or bookmarks printed with your book's sleeve cover on the front. You can sign these for the staff as a thank you – a gesture that will go a long way to getting you booked again. Pack a decent digital camera to take some publicity shots of the signing – take as many as you can with customers and staff. Be sure to also forward these to your agent and publicist. If you're in a small, independent book store always take the time to buy something – they've been good enough to support you, so be sure to return the favour.

❛ALWAYS READY TO PACK – AND GO

An Expert's View...

Would I be able to leave for South America next week? Why certainly!

There was a time in my life when such requests would have seemed completely inconceivable, but over the years I've been steadily developing a whole new level of flexibility. If adventure knocks, I usually open the door with a resounding yes. Of course it helps if you have no partner, family, friends or pets to repeatedly let down, or even better, a very understanding, long-suffering bunch of the above, used to your globetrotting ways. Packing fast and being prepared to jet off when opportunity presents itself are key skills for a travel writer and even more so in these times of fiercer competition and tighter budgets. And could I head for Amsterdam straight after Colombia? Sure, no worries.

Anna Maria Espsäter is a London-based freelance travel and food writer hailing from Sweden. For the last 20 years she's been roaming the globe, visiting over 80 countries. She specialises in Latin America and Scandinavia.

(Visit: www.annamariaespsater.co.uk)

Appendix 1

Glossary

About the author: Usually a paragraph or two of relevant information about the author. Used for books, book proposals, articles and websites. Written in the third person.

Adjective: An adjective modifies a noun or a pronoun by describing, identifying, or quantifying words. An adjective usually precedes the noun or the pronoun which it modifies. For example,'a *battered* music box sat on the mahogany sideboard'.

Advance: A publishing term for money paid to an author before the book is published. Usually calculated on estimated book sales.

Adverb: An adverb can modify a verb or an adjective, another adverb, a phrase or a clause. It answers questions such as 'how', 'where', 'when' and 'how much' and indicates manner, time, place and cause. For example, 'The medics waited *nervously* for the first signs of life'.

Advertorial: Combining the words 'editorial' and 'advertisement', an advertorial refers to a type of print advertisement designed to resemble editorial content. Although it is written in the form of an objective opinion editorial (and may resemble a news story about a product or service) it is a paid placement like any other form of advertising in a magazine, newspaper, or other printed publication, but is a less obvious form of advertisement than traditional ads.

Agent: A professional representative engaged by the writer or author to market creative works to editors and publishing houses.

All rights: A legal term to describe the ownership of the rights to the work.

Alliteration: A series of words in a sentence all beginning with the same sound.

Analogy: Use of two dissimilar things as a comparison to explain or illustrate a concept.

Anaphora: Use of several consecutive sentences starting with the same group of words (i.e., 'I didn't blink. I didn't breathe. I didn't swallow.').

Angle (slant): The bias with which the author presents the information in an article (the angle from which the subject is tackled).

Anthology: Collection of creative works written by various authors published as a compilation.

Antonyms: Opposites (clean vs. dirty; bad vs. good).

Appendix: Supplementary materials printed at the end of the general text.

Assignment: A commissioned work by an editor or publisher.

Attachments: Files (documents, video clips, audio clips or photographs) that are attached to an email (electronic) message.

Audience: Describes the readership most likely to be interested in the subject matter of a particular book or publication.

Author guidelines: Guidelines provided by a publication or publisher that explains how to submit pitches, articles or completed manuscripts for consideration.

Autobiography: A self-written life story (different from a biography, when an author writes about someone else's life).

B2B: Business to business; describes a business whose primary customers are other businesses.

B2C: Business to customer; describes a business whose primary customers are individuals.

Backlist: A list of books published before the current publishing year, but still in print.

Bad debts: An accounting term, bad debts are outstanding monies (receivables) that exceed the normal, acceptable time for payment and prove difficult, or impossible, to collect.

Bibliography: A list of resources used in the process of writing a book, article, report or paper (people, books, magazines, websites and other sources of information).

Bimonthly: Every two months (used when referring to a magazine that publishes every second month, six times a year).

Bio: A short description of the writer in the third person (used to accompany articles), sometimes including contacts (web, email, etc.).

Biography: A life story of someone other than the writer.

Biweekly: Every two weeks (used when referring to a twice-monthly title).

Blank verse: Poetry that doesn't rhyme.

Blog: Shortened from the term 'weblog', blogs are websites that are usually maintained by an individual that display regular entries of commentary (postings) that are often descriptions of events commonly displayed in reverse-chronological order. Travel blogs typically combine text, images, and links to other blogging travellers.

Blogger: A person who writes a **blog**.

Book launch: An event or party that serves as the official launch of a new book. Usually includes everyone involved in the process (author, publisher, project manager, editor) plus a list of invited guests and press.

Book review: A published review or summary of a book.

Book tour: A series of trade events, press briefings and consumer-facing activities that promote and publicise a book and raise the profile of the author.

Box-out: A small body of text separate to the main editorial, often used to expand on something mentioned in passing or referred to. Can also be a way of breaking up large bodies of text.

Brainstorming: Collecting lots of ideas on a subject, usually by exchanging ideas with others but can be undertaken alone.

Byline: An author's name appearing with his or her published work.

Caption: A description of a photograph, graph, table or diagram.

Chapters: Sections that form the compositions of the main content of a book.

Classified section: A section of a newspaper or some magazines that are wholly dedicated to advertising, usually in the form of smaller ads to maximise revenue.

Cliché: An overused expression or descriptive term.

Click-throughs: A term to describe the proportion of website traffic that move from one site straight to another site using click-through links. CTR (click-through-rate) is a way of measuring the success of an online marketing by calculating the number of users who clicked through by the number of time the image or icon was delivered.

Clips (or cuttings): Examples of published writing used to demonstrate ability, style and credentials to potential clients.

Closing paragraph: Final paragraph (that concludes the end of an article).

Closing sentence: Final sentence (that concludes the end of an article and a final paragraph).

Collaboration: A process where two or more people or organisations work together in an intersection of common goals – for example, an online travel blog or co-authorship.

Colour section: A publishing term for the part of a book where full-colour is used, usually for photographs.

Column inch: Refers to imperial measurement used in newspapers that measures content (1 column wide × 1 inch long).

Columnist: A writer, often a journalist, who writes for publication in a series, creating copy that offers strong opinion. Columns appear in newspapers, magazine and other publications, including blogs and e-zines.

Commission: An assignment awarded to a writer, author or photographer which specifies the style of work requested and content. Sometimes supplied in written form (as a contract) but often a verbal agreement.

Commissioning editor: The person responsible for commissioning work and content by writers and author in a magazine, publisher, newspaper or for an online resource.

Compound sentence: Two or more sentences linked together using the words 'and', 'but', or 'or'.

Consumer press: Publications targeting a particular consumer group.

Contents: A listing in magazines, newspapers and books that outlines what order or structure the editorial content is in (usually with page numbers for ease of reference).

Contract: A legally binding agreement issued by publishers to writers and authors that covers the terms and conditions of the work outlined.

Copy: Refers to any text that needs to be written in publishing, from articles and books to adverts and brochures. Also refers to the main text of a story in news circles.

Copyediting: Checking for errors in spelling, grammar, punctuation and word usage in writing content.

Copyright: The ownership by an author of his or her works.

Courtesy copy: A complimentary copy of a magazine, book, newspaper or other printed matter, usually when some or all of the written content relates in some way to the recipient.

Cover art: The design of the book jacket, using images and/or words.

Coverage: A term used by PR agencies to describe the amount of editorial press space allocated to their client, often as a result of issuing press releases or hosting a press trip.

Covering letter: A short introductory letter to editors and publishers that accompanies a pitch and samples of published works or a completed article, novel, non-fiction book manuscript, or a resumé.

Creative writing: Any writing, fiction, poetry, non-fiction (including travel writing) that falls outside the bounds of journalistic, technical and academic literature.

Credit control: The management of payments due in (receivables) to ensure prompt collection and smooth cashflow.

Credits: An author's or writer's list of publications.

Crosshead: A few words used to break up large amounts of text in a feature (these are normally taken from the main text).

Cut: A term that refers to reducing or reshaping copy, normally to lower the word-count.

Cuttings: Samples of publishing works (once cut out of a magazine or newspaper, but now usually scanned into PDF electronic form).

Daily rate: The fee charged by a writer or author per day.

Deadline: The final date/time for the submission of an assignment.

Dead metaphor: A metaphor that has lost its intended intensity through overuse.

Descriptive paragraph: A paragraph that describes a person, a place, a feeling or an idea.

Destination piece: A piece of writing that explores a place within the structure of a theme or angle but offers a broad overview nonetheless.

Dialogue: The use of speech within a story, usually denoted by quotation marks.

Digital photography: Photography using a digital camera with images produced in digital form.

Direct quote: The exact reproduction of a verbatim quote in quote-marks and correctly attributed.

Distributor: A company that buys books in bulk from a publisher or other distributors and resells them to retail accounts.

Double spacing: Refers to the space format on a page of word-processed (or typed) copy.

Download: A document, audio clip, software program, photograph or video retrievable electronically from the internet.

Dummy: A rough (often hand-drawn) mock-up of how a page or a publication is shaping up (usually used for space allocation).

E-commerce: Shopping facility online with electronic payment.

Edit: The review of a piece of writing for correction purposes (grammar, spelling, sense and style and other errors and inconsistencies) together with an overall critique.

Editing: The process of reviewing a piece of writing and making corrections. Also see **Edit**.

Editor: A skilled professional commissioned to check a work for grammar, spelling and typographical errors as well as issues with the content, such as style and consistency.

Electronic submission: A submission of content by email.

Embargo: Restriction on publishing information released to reporters until a specific date or time (usually to ensure that all news outlets release the story on the same day).

Emerging destinations: Countries (or regions, places or specific resort areas) that are upcoming in popularity.

Endnote: Text written at the end of an article stating the author's credentials.

Essay: A group of paragraphs that present facts and analysis about one main idea.

Expository paragraph: A paragraph that provides information on a topic, or steps explaining how to do something.

E-zine: Electronic format internet magazine.

Fact checker: A person who checks factual assertions in non-fictional text, usually intended for publication to determine their veracity and correctness.

Fair use: A term used to describe the reproduction of short excerpts from a copyrighted work, usually for educational or review purposes.

Feature: Although the term 'feature' implies softer news, a feature is often defined by its length and style and appears in the middle of a magazine or newspaper.

Fees: The money paid to authors, writers and photographers for their works (for example: by the word, by the hour, or a single flat fee).

Final draft: The last copy of the manuscript after all other proofing and editing steps have been completed.

First draft: Also called **rough draft**. The first organised version of a piece of work.

First Electronic Rights: The right to publish a piece of writing electronically for the first time. Once First Electronic Rights have been assigned to a given piece of writing, this work cannot be published in another electronic medium.

First Print Rights: The rights anywhere in the world to a piece of writing in print.

Flatplan: Similar to a **dummy**, a flatplan is a page-by-page plan that shows where the articles and adverts are laid out.

Follow-up: A polite letter, email or telephone call to establish the status of an earlier query, pitch or manuscript submission.

Format: The manner and style in which content is prepared and presented.

Forward feature list: A schedule of planned features that includes dates (deadline and production), content, angle and theme.

Freelance(r): A self-employed person with no particular long-term commitment to a single employer.

Genre: A specific category of literature, marked by a distinctive style, form or content.

Go-ahead: A positive response to a query letter that assigns an article to you.

Grammar: The rules of a language.

Guidelines: Instructions for submitting work to a publication for consideration.

Hard copy: A print out of the manuscript.

High resolution: High resolution refers to an image reproduced with a high level of detail, usually in photographic form (often digital). A high resolution digital image is a minimum of 300 dpi and around 1MB in size. More mega pixels in an image usually means a higher quality resolution.

Homographs: Words that are spelled alike but pronounced differently and/or have different meanings.

Homonyms: Words that are spelled and pronounced alike but have different meanings (for example 'bash' – a strike or blow, and 'bash' – a party).

Hook: A narrative trick or engaging attention-grabber at the beginning of a creative work (lead paragraph or first page of book) that draws the reader in and keeps them reading.

Hourly rate: The per-hour fee charged by an author or writer.

House-style: A publication's guide to style, spelling and use of grammar, designed to help writers and authors submit work in a consistent way for their target audience.

How-to: An article that provides step-by-step information or directions on how to make or do something.

Hyperbole: Deliberate exaggeration (often used in the short form, 'hype').

Image library: Photographic resource offered to the media by companies, organisations, PR agencies and promotional departments (often online in downloadable digital form).

Impartiality: Objective writing without bias.

Imprint: A division within a publishing house that deals with a specific category of books.

Index: An extensive list of key words or phrases ('headings') and associated pointers ('locators') in a book that directs the reader to specific content by stating page number.

Interview: To question a person or a group about their lives, experiences, opinions or area of expertise.

Invoice: A document issued for payment (submitted to an accounts department).

Journal: A diary or record of events, feelings and thoughts, usually recorded by date. It can take many forms.

Journey piece: The same as a **travelogue**. An editorial that conveys the experience of journeying using descriptive narrative.

Kicker: The first sentence or first few words of a story's lead, set in a font size larger than the body text of the story.

Kill fee: Payment given to an author if a magazine cannot or will not use an article assigned to the author (often 50% of the original agreed fee).

Lead: The first paragraph of a manuscript or article, usually includes a 'hook' to draw the reader in.

Lead time: The time between the commission and publication of the article.

Low resolution: Refers to a digital photograph that has a small amount of pixels, causing the image to be of lower quality and not suitable for printed matter (but ideal for use on the web).

Magazines: Periodicals that usually contain a miscellaneous collection of articles, stories, poems, and pictures. Usually published in glossy, full-colour for specific reader groups, both for trade and consumer sectors.

Manuscript: The author's copy of a novel, non-fiction book, screenplay or article. Usually a word processed document (but could be typed or hand-written).

Market research: Studies and evaluation that discover what people want, need, believe or how they act. Once that research is completed, it can be used to determine how to market your product.

Marketing campaign: A specific marketing project with a clearly defined set of targets and goals.

Marketing data: Intelligence of varying types that allows a business to understand certain aspects of a market.

Marketing tools: Technology, objects and printed matter used to effect a marketing campaign.

Markets: Places to do business.

Masthead: List of information about the newspaper or the magazine itself (publisher, editor and staff) included in every issue, typically printed on the inside cover.

Memoirs: (From the French *mémoire*, from the Latin *memoria*, meaning 'memory', or a reminiscence) a subclass of autobiography that usually takes the form of a collection of recollections.

Mentor: An experienced (and usually trusted, motivational or inspirational) person who advises and guides a less-experienced member of their profession as they advance.

Metaphor: Language that indicates a similarity between two different things without the use of the words 'like' or 'as', for example, 'the sun was a egg yolk'. Compare with **simile**.

Meter: The rhythm or pattern of syllables (usually in poetry).

Mixed metaphor: Confusing two common metaphors.

Moral: The lesson in a story.

Narrative: A paragraph or piece of work that tells a story.

Narrator: The person or character who tells and explains a story.

Networking: A group of people who exchange information, contacts, and experience for professional or social purposes.

News peg: A story that 'hangs' on a newsy hook.

Novel: A work of fiction (usually 45,000 words or more).

Observation: A description of the physical characteristics or behaviour of a person, place or object to convey the look, feel, smell, sounds and taste to the reader.

Off-the-record: Information that must not be disclosed.

On acceptance: Term that relates to the payment received by a writer or author only after the editor accepts the finished works.

On publication: Term that relates to the payment received by a writer or author only once the works have been published.

On spec: When a writer submits a piece speculatively.

Online content: Copy, images and other material used on the internet.

Onomatopoeia: Words that sound like, imitate or evoke their meaning, i.e., hiss, slush or slither.

Outline: A brief description of the major ideas or content in a written work.

Over-matter: Copy (text and images) that is too much for the allocated space.

Over-on-words: Refers to an article or manuscript that exceeds the specific word count as detailed in the brief.

Overview: Description (usually one or two pages) of a book idea intended to introduce the work to a publisher.

Oxymoron: A phrase composed of two words with contradictory meanings, such as 'definite maybe'.

Paragraph: A group of sentences that discuss one main subject. There are four basic types of paragraphs: (1) descriptive, (2) narrative, (3) persuasive, and (4) expository.

Payment: An agreed amount of money for a piece of work.

PB: An abbreviation for 'picture book'.

Personal essay: An essay written in the first person.

Personification: Attributing human characteristics to a non-human object, place or event.

Persuasive paragraph: A paragraph that states an opinion and tries to persuade the reader to agree.

Photo-blogging: Contributing photographs to a blog.

Pitch: Putting forward an idea for a story or book to a publisher or editor.

Plagiarism: Presenting another author's works, words, or ideas as one's own.

Plot: The main, central events of a story.

Podcast: MP3 audio recordings that can automatically download to a user's computer as soon as they are published online.

Prefix: An affix which is placed before the stem of a word (for example, 'sub' or 'over').

Prelims: Pages at the beginning of a book that include rights information, publisher information, foreword, contents list, acknowledgements and a list of illustrations.

Press pack/press kit: Material available to writers, journalists and the press in general about a product, service, company (usually including a press release, CD of images, feature ideas and information).

Press release: A short written or recorded communication issued by PR companies and departments directed at members of the media for the purposes of raising awareness of an event, product or company.

Press trip: An organised media trip by a travel company, hotel chain, airline, tour operator or tourist board in which travel journalists, writers and authors are familiarised with the product (destination, hotel, resort, new flight route, etc.), usually without charge.

Project manager: Person who takes the manuscript from submission stage to publication, working closely with the author or writer(s).

Proofreading: Close examination of a piece of work to identify and correct mistakes.

Proposal: A summary of a proposed book that is used to sell the idea to a publisher or editor.

Public domain: Material that can be freely used by the public, and does not come under the protection of a copyright, trademark, or patent.

Public Lending Rights (PLR): Looks after the rights of authors, photographers and writers in relation to government-run public libraries.

Public relations (PR): Refers to the role of publicity and promotion, an interface between the company or product and the press.

Publishing director: The person responsible for developing the publishing list of titles and overseeing the editorial function.

Pull-out quote: A selected quote from a story highlighted next to the main text. Often used in interviews.

Quality press: A category of newspapers in national circulation in the UK distinguished by their seriousness.

Referrals: Similar to recommendations with clients (or colleagues) suggesting you to others as a source of supply.

Rejection: A negative response from an editor or publisher that indicates they are not interested in the submitted work or idea (pitch).

Report writing: Compiling factual information in document form to a specific brief to fulfil a clearly defined structure and purpose.

Representation: Someone who works on your behalf, often representing your interests in contractual negotiations and new business discussions.

Reprints: When books are printed to fulfil demand or when previously published articles are made available for publication in other magazines or journals.

Retainer: Regular payments (or one-off annual fee) that is held as a 'deposit' against future invoices to secure a writer or author on a retained basis.

Review copy: A free copy of a book given away to the press to be reviewed.

Revisions: Changes that improve writing.

Rights: Legal information about who retains control over all the various ways in which a creative work may be reproduced, used, or applied.

Rough draft: The first organised version of a piece of work.

Round-up: Also called service stories, a round-up provides readers with a practical overview of specific destination or travel-related topic, often as how-to articles, Top 10 beaches, resort reviews and the latest travel news.

Royalties: Moneys paid to an author based on book sales and calculated as a percentage of the cover price.

Royalty free: Content licensed under a set of guidelines that allows the licensee to use it freely in perpetuity without paying additional royalty charges.

Run: To print an article.

Running copy: Sentences without punctuation or connecting words. Can also refer to free-flowing, longer paragraphs.

SAE: Abbreviation for stamped self-addressed envelope (often used when sending out manuscripts).

Self publishing: Distinct area of publishing that provides a way for authors to publish their own works (but unsupported by distribution, sales, promotion and marketing).

Sentence fragment: A sentence that is missing the subject, the verb, or both.

Side bar (side panel): Extra information, practical hints and tips in a separate box or bar attached to the main body of the article.

Simile: Comparing two different things using the words 'like' or 'as'. For example, 'her eyes were like dewy grass'.

Simultaneous submission: Submitting the same manuscript and pitches to many editors and publishers at once.

Slush pile: A term for unsolicited manuscripts received by a publisher or editor.

Special interest article: A piece written for inclusion in a title aimed at a particular, specialist group of readers.

Spin-off: A new product or development that is spawned from an original idea.

Spread: Also called a double-page spread (DPS), a spread is two facing pages.

Staff writer: An in-house, employed status writer.

Stand-fast: Line of text immediately under the title/headline that gives the reader more information on what the article is about.

Subject: The main topic in a piece of writing. (It can be in a sentence, paragraph, an essay or book.)

Submission guidelines: Guidelines provided by a publication that explains how to submit pitches, articles or completed manuscripts for consideration.

Suffix: An affix that is placed after the stem of a word (for example 'ful' or 'ship').

Summary: A short description of the main ideas in a body of work.

Supplement: A special publication published in conjunction, as a secondary format, to a larger title.

Syndication: Editorial content sold for multiple use in different publications.

Synonyms: Words that have approximately the same meaning, for example, 'little' and 'small'.

Synopsis: An abbreviated description of a book or manuscript sent to the publisher covering all the main points of the work.

Tabloid press: Smaller newspaper format.

Tagline/strapline: Memorable, attention-grabbing text used in marketing and promotion.

Terms and conditions (T&C): T&Cs specify the terms of a particular work, from the types of rights purchased and expected date of publication to the payment schedule.

Thumbnails: Small, reduced-sized low resolution images that allow easy review in multiples.

Time management: The effective management of time in order to maximise profitability and productivity.

Topic sentences: Usually at the beginning of a paragraph, the sentence includes the main idea of the paragraph.

Tourist board: A state-funded organisation responsible for the promotion and development of tourism.

Trade press: Publications targeting a particular occupation or industry.

Traffic: The amount of users recorded by a website.

Travel guidebooks: Guidebook to a specific place, region or destination.

Travelogue: Another name for a **journey piece**.

Unique selling point (USP): The qualities that make a business distinct from others.

Unsolicited manuscripts: An article, story or book that a publication did not request.

Vanity publishing: The publishing sector that provides an author with a paid-for way to publish their work.

Verb: The word in a sentence that indicates action.

Voice: The tone, style and method with which the writer composes a piece of work.

Web TV: Internet TV stations and video feeds.

Widows and orphans: A publishing term for the last line of a paragraph, printed alone at the top of a page (widow) and the first line of a paragraph, printed alone at the bottom of a page (orphan). Both spoil the look of printed matter.

Withdrawal letter: A letter from the writer or author to the publisher or editor withdrawing a manuscript from consideration.

Word count: The specified length of an article or manuscript.

Writer guidelines: Guidelines provided by a publication that explains how to submit pitches, articles or completed manuscripts for consideration.

Writer's block: A period of time when writers are unable to write for creative reasons, usually as a result of a lack of any good ideas or a crisis of confidence.

Appendix 2

Directory

CREATIVE WRITING COURSES

Arvon Foundation Ltd
Professional creative writing courses run throughout UK venues.
Tel: 020 7324 2554. www.arvonfoundation.org

Bradt Travel Guides
This most respected of independent travel publishers has an
equally renowned calendar of annual travel writing seminars to
its name in which it explores destination writing from
Antarctica to Zanzibar and much more besides.
www.bradt-travelguides.com

British College of Journalism
Freelance distance-learning journalism course that focuses as
much on getting paid as guiding writers to develop their skills.
www.britishcollegeofjournalism.com

British Guild of Travel Writers
The British Guild of Travel Writers is the association of
Britain's top professional travel journalists, guidebook writers,
photographers, broadcasters and travel editors and runs an
impressive range of high-quality professional courses throughout
the year. www.bgtw.org (see also: Memberships, Guilds and
Associations on page 248).

International Travel Writers Alliance
UK-run organisation with a global reach that sometimes runs
training and educational events for its members in partnership
with a wide range of travel industry partners and agencies.
www.internationaltravelwritersalliance.com.

Kingston University London

Runs occasional travel writing workshops along with an MA course in creative writing and publishing. www.kingston.ac.uk

Lancaster University

Has a sizeable creative writing programme that includes travel writing and an MA course. Tel: 01524 65201. www.lancs.ac.uk

London School of Journalism

Distance-learning, full-time courses in London and occasional workshops. www.lsj.org

Mary Ward Centre

Runs regular creative writing courses, including travel writing. Tel: 020 7269 6000. www.marywardcentre.ac.uk

Media Bistro

Organises several affordable Travel Writing Boot Camps annually, mostly in Latin America. www.mediabistro.com

National Union of Journalists

The NUJ runs a variety of training courses including those aimed specifically at freelance writers. www.nuj.org.uk

New York University

Founded in 1831, NYU runs occasional travel writing seminars as well as creative writing courses and non-fiction workshops. www.nyu.edu

Oxford University

Impressive creative programme with undergraduate, postgraduate and short-course options. www.ox.ac.uk

PMA Training

Runs a range of journalism courses, including a number of travel writing options. Tel: 01480 300653. www.pma-group.com

Society of American Travel Writers

The professional association of North American travel writers, journalists, photographers and other travel industry media members runs regular training courses and skills updates. www.satw.org

Society of Women Writers and Journalists

The UK's oldest association for professional women writers and journalists (established in 1894) runs several workshops and seminars throughout the year. www.swwj.co.uk

Sydney Writers' Centre

Runs a diverse array of short-term courses for writers working in all genres, from travel and fiction to poetry. www.sydneywriterscentre.com.au

Travel and Type

Portal of UK writing workshops and sources, including those specifically for aspiring travel authors and journalists. www.travelandtype.com

Travel Workshops

Regular full-day workshops run with guest speakers from the national press, such as award-winning journalist Dea Birkett and renowned author Rory Maclean. www.travelworkshops.co.uk

Travellers' Tales

High-quality travel writing courses in Spain, Turkey, Morocco and London run by a dedicated team of many of the UK's most experienced travel writing professionals. www.travellerstales.org

University of East Anglia

Full-time and part-time creative writing study options involving a much-acclaimed programme of guest speakers from the travel writing and publishing scene. www.uea.ac.uk

Westminster Kingsway College

Runs a range of creative writing courses including those aimed specifically at women together with workshops for writers aged 60+ and general travel writing training. www.westking.ac.uk

Women On Tour

Creative writing courses run by a friendly networking community of women in Istanbul, Barcelona and London (with tentative future plans to expand into South America). Women On Tour aims to boost the confidence of creative women and to support their goals, aims and dreams through mutual understanding and shared experiences. www.womenontour.co.uk

Writing Classes

America online resource for creative writing courses in NY State – and beyond. www.writingclasses.com

Writing on the Road

US-based organisation set up to teach travel writing in a real-world setting, such as Central America, with week-long courses that cover the business-side of pitching and freelancing as well as how to be a travel writer on the road. www.writingontheroad.com

SELF-EMPLOYED/FREELANCE

Building Your Own Business: How to be Your Own Boss by Creating Your Own Business or Going Freelance, John Hawkins (The Crowood Press Ltd).

Byliners: 101 Ways to be a Freelance Journalist, Cedric Pulford (Ituri Publications).

Freelance Writing for Newspapers, Jill Dick (A & C Black Publishers Ltd; 3rd rev. edn.).

Get Paid to Write! The No-Nonsense Guide to Freelance Writing, Thomas Williams (Sentient Publications).

Getting Started as a Freelance Writer, Robert W Bly (Sentient Publications; rev. and expanded edn.).

Go Freelance: How to Succeed at Being Your Own Boss (Steps to Success) (A & C Black Publishers Ltd).

Go It Alone: The Streetwise Secrets of Self-employment, Geoff Burch (Capstone Publishing).

Make a Real Living as a Freelance Writer: How to Win Top Writing Assignments, Jenna Glatzer (Nomad Press).

No Contacts? No Problem! How to Pitch and Sell Your Freelance Feature Writing, Catherine Quinn (Methuen Drama).

Renegade Writer: A Totally Unconventional Guide to Freelance Writing Success, Linda Formichelli and Diana Burrell (Marion Street Press Inc.; 2nd rev. edn.).

Starting Your Career As a Freelance Writer, Moira Allen (Allworth Press).

Successfully Going Freelance in a Week, Brian Holmes (Hodder & Stoughton Ltd; 2nd rev. edn.).

The Freelance Writer's Handbook: How to Make Money and Enjoy Your Life, Andrew Crofts (Piatkus Books; 3rd rev. edn.).

The Freelance Writer's Handbook: How to Turn Your Writing Skills into a Successful Business, Andrew Crofts (Piatkus Books).

The Greatest Freelance Writing Tips in the World, Linda Jones (The Greatest in the World Limited).

The Principles of Successful Freelancing, Miles Burke (Sitepoint; illustrated edn.).

MEMBERSHIPS, GUILDS AND ASSOCIATIONS

American Society of Journalists and Authors

Founded in 1948, this highly proactive membership organisation campaigns on issues of standards, payment and rights. It publishes an informative online magazine and runs a freelance search database and maintains a presence on every social networking site. For membership details visit the website. (An annual fee applies.) www.asja.org

Australian Society of Travel Writers

Dedicated to protecting the rights and serving the interests of its members and reporting on the travel industry, the Australian Society of Travel Writers boasts a growing number of members from all areas of travel writing. It also hosts an annual awards event, regular networking and social soirees and serves as the voice of the industry down-under. An annual fee applies (with various membership categories). www.astw.org.au

Chartered Institute of Journalists (CIOJ)

Founded in 1808, the CIOJ was granted its royal charter in 1890, and is a leading membership organisation within the UK's media industry. Freelance journalists have always formed a significant part of the membership: a separate section for them was set up in 1943 and they are now one of the largest groups in the Institute. Other groups include sections for travel writers, motoring journalists, public relations and a history and heritage writers' section. An annual fee applies. www.cioj.co.uk

Editorial Freelancers Association (EFA)

US-based national professional organisation established in 1970 dedicated to supporting freelance workers within the editorial sector. EFA members are editors, writers, indexers, proofreaders, researchers, desktop publishers, translators, and others who offer a broad range of skills and specialities. The HQ is in New York with regional offices US-wide that offer client outreach seminars, a job listing subscription service, networking with peers online, at meetings, and at social events, educational programmes designed especially for freelancers, a bimonthly newsletter and other publications, comprehensive health insurance (where available) and a searchable, online membership directory. An annual fee applies. www.the-efa.org

International Travel Writers Alliance

This far-reaching collective is open to anyone connected within the travel industry and as such has no eligibility stipulation other than that. Expect to hook up with travel agents, writers, editors and photographers in some of the Alliance's virtual networking events. It also produces a summary of travel industry news for its broadcaster, writer and photographer members. Membership is offered via an annual fee. www.internationaltravelwritersalliance.com

International Travel Writers & Photographers Alliance (ITWPA)

This professional network of travel writers and photographers hails from around the globe. It publishes a well-read magazine *Travel Post Monthly* and hosts an imaginative collection of events to bring like-minded professionals together. Other benefits include providing members with educational opportunities to enhance their travel writing and photography skills whilst also sharpening their marketing expertise. An annual fee applies. www.itwpa.com

Midwest Travel Writers Association (MTWA)

With a membership that spans travel writers, authors, broadcasters and publicity groups and PR agencies, MTWA represents the 13 Midwestern states: Illinois, Indiana, Iowa, Kansas, Kentucky, Michigan, Minnesota, Missouri, Nebraska, North Dakota, Ohio, South Dakota and Wisconsin. Membership criteria vary so check the website for details of current fees and eligibility. www.mtwa.org

National Association of Women Writers (NAWW)

Founded in 2001, the NAWW comprises 3,000 members worldwide. It aims to help connect and educate members through online shared tips and advice on how to get published, sell and benefit from a writing career. It publishes a range of 'How To' books and CDs and hosts tele-events and physical chapter events and circulates a weekly newsletter. An annual fee applies. www.naww.org

North American Travel Journalists Association (NATJA)

With the largest single membership of travel writing specialists, the NATJA is one of the biggest collectives of professional travel editors, journalists, writers, authors and photographers. It hosts an annual well-attended conference and seminars and was founded in 1991 by New Jersey travel writers Bob Nesoff and Dan Schlossberg. To join NATJA, applicants must prove only that they are legitimate working travel journalists – it currently has more than 500 members and charges an annual membership fee. www.natja.org

National Union Journalists (NUJ)

The largest journalists' union in the world with over 40,000 members, the NUJ also has thousands of freelance members who belong to its wide variety of branches and networks. It has a strong tradition of campaigning on behalf of its members on issues of pay and conditions, protecting their rights and expanding their skills through UK-wide courses and training seminars. An annual fee applies. www.nuj.org.uk

Outdoors Writers Association of America (OWAA)

OWAA is an international, professional association of outdoor communicators, outdoor companies and outdoor industry service providers in the US. It runs an annual awards programme, networking events and is 'the voice' of outdoor specialists in America. www.owaa.org

Outdoor Writers' Guild

Established in 1980, the Outdoor Writers' Guild is open to writers, journalists, authors, photographers, illustrators, broadcasters, film-makers and creative artists in the UK and Ireland. www.owg.org.uk

Pacific Asia Travel Writers Associations (PATWA)

Created to represent all the agencies involved in the travel and tourism industry, Delhi-based PATWA organises a number of regional meetings and conferences that allow travel professionals to exchange ideas, experiences, and disseminate information about new developments in their respective areas of activity. It publishes a newsletter and campaigns to maintain high standards of professionalism in travel communication in conjunction with the Fundamental Principles of the UNESCO and of the World Organization of Tourism. www.patwainternational.com

Society of American Travel Writers (SATW)

SATW is the world's largest association of professional travel journalists and photographers with over 700 active members, all of whom produce a substantial amount of travel journalism to qualify as members. The society also has over 400 associate members, public relations professionals representing the world's top destinations, hotels, airlines, attractions and resorts. SATW is divided into five regional areas throughout the US and Canada. Check the website for fees and application details. www.satw.org

Society of Authors (UK)

This highly-respected organisation works to protect the rights and further the interests of authors in the United Kingdom. It runs well-attended 'meet the members' events and has a website packed with FAQs, membership information and news. Founded over a century ago, the Society of Authors has more than 8,500 members writing in all areas of the profession. Whatever your specialisation, from novelists to doctors, textbook writers to ghost writers, broadcasters to academics, illustrators to translators, you are eligible as a member as soon as you have been offered a contract. Fees are paid annually and there is a regular newsletter. www.societyofauthors.org

Society of Women Writers and Journalists

The UK's oldest society for professional women writers was founded in 1894 by newspaper proprietor Joseph Snell Wood. Today, the SWWJ has grown to become an international association, and is affiliated to women's associations worldwide. In 2004, the Society took the decision to invite men who are published writers to join them as associate members. It aims to encourage literary achievement, uphold professional standards, and enable social contact with fellow writers and others in the field, including editors, publishers, broadcasters and agents. Many of the SWWJ's meetings are held at The Writers' House, 13 Haydon Street, London EC3N 1DB. Regular events include workshops, visits to places of literary interest, an annual Country Members Day, Autumn Lunch, and Christmas get-

together, all of which include big-name guest speakers, a
biennial residential Weekend Conference featuring talks,
discussions, and seminars on a wide variety of topics, plus
biennial overseas trips. It offers five different levels of
membership for an annual fee – all details and eligibility
requirements can be found on the website. www.swwj.co.u

The British Guild of Travel Writers

Has a membership of several hundred that includes some of
Britain's top professional travel journalists, guidebook writers,
photographers, broadcasters and travel editors. Eligibility is
assessed on a case-by-case basis with applicants required to
demonstrate a minimum level of published work. Benefits
include networking events, discounted goods and services (such
as insurances, travel equipment, airport parking and transport),
newsletter and an extremely well-run annual awards event. It
also issues an email bulletin to commissioning editors full of
news about what members are doing – a highly effective
marketing tool. It offers two types of memberships for an
annual fee. Check the website for full details of applications and
membership benefits. www.bgtw.org

**The International Food Wine and Travel Writers Association
(IFWTWA)**

Founded in 1956 by a group of professional food, wine and
travel writers in Paris, the IFWTWA is now an international
membership organisation with headquarters in the United
States. Today, its membership has grown to include writers,
authors, photographers and broadcasters (mostly domestic and
several international) across a broad spectrum of travel
destination attractions such as active and passive adventure
activities, ecology, historical features, culture, fairs, festivals and
special events. IFWTWA includes professionals in the culinary
arts and sciences, the wine growing and production industry,
and in the hotel and hospitality management industries. It

organises conferences, regional meetings, and press/media trips
and runs a scholarship. For eligibility criteria and membership
fees see the website. www.ifwtwa.org

Travel Media Association of Canada (TMAC)

Founded in 1994 by Isobel Warren, a long-standing Canadian
travel journalist and author, TMAC currently has about 500
members across the travel communications sector, from writers,
journalists and authors to specialist PR agencies.
www.travelmedia.ca

Women On Tour

This friendly all-female networking community runs regular
events in Istanbul, Barcelona and London (with tentative future
plans to expand into South America) and includes a number of
writers and publishers. www.womenontour.co.uk

Writers Union of Canada

This national organisation represents thousands of writing
professionals and is proactive in campaigning for rights and
conditions. Members' benefits include access to programmes
which provide income assistance to writers, professional
development, professional assistance, and access to other
writers. While providing members with programmes to assist
them the Union is also advocating on behalf of writers, with the
creation of Public Lending Right and Access Copyright
programmes that provide much needed income for writers a
notable recent success. The Union is currently lobbying to
reform income tax laws to ensure fairness for writers; ensure
that provincial Status of the Artist legislation is introduced
which includes a well-worded labour relations component;
ensure that new copyright legislation reflects the views and
needs of creators; implement programmes to increase writers'
incomes; and defend the freedom to write and publish. An
annual fee applies. www.writersunion.ca

TRAVEL WRITING HOLIDAYS

Artemisia Holidays

Italian holidays, art holidays and writing courses take place in the lively mediaeval walled city of Barga in Tuscany where flexible programmes offer plenty of 'down time' within a small group environment. Tailormade programmes promise everything from inspiration to resolving writers' block so that participants leave with happy memories of friends made, images of the sights seen and the sense of achievement in having developing that manuscript idea. www.artemisia-holidays.com

Creative Escapes

Offering inspirational and enlightening travel-writing courses in France, Spain, Morocco and Norway, Creative Escapes engages a highly impressive group of authors and photographers as part of its tutoring team. Apart from the learning, which often takes place by the pool or under the shade of a giant fig tree, Creative Escapes actively explores and observes the locale, allowing participants to wander around a medieval market, taste wine in local bodegas, dip their feet in the sea and salsa the night away in a local bar – all as part of their research for their writing. Friendly, instructive and interactive lessons allow individuals to develop their own style and ideas at a relaxed pace. www.creative-escapes.co.uk

Skyros

Skyros was established in 1979 and is now Europe's leading provider of alternative holidays – it's 'the first and still the best' according to *The Guardian*. Part of its holistic approach in offering holidays that engage the individual in activities and events that open the heart and expand the mind, is The Writers' Lab held on the beautiful Greek island of Skyros. This writing holiday programme is famous for kick-starting writing careers with the help of distinguished authors including Booker Prize winners or nominees. The benefits of a Skyros holiday last long after the suntan has faded. They include new friendships and relationships, new interests, a fresh outlook or a new sense of direction and attract people from all over the world. Although all ages are represented, from five to 85, approximately 70% of all participants are aged 30–50. The sense of renewed confidence and excitement about life is palpable. Poet Hugo Williams described Skyros as the holiday 'you can take home with you'. www.skyros.co.uk

Travellers' Tales

Travellers' Tales offers a range of travel writing holidays in inspirational settings in Turkey, Morocco, Spain and the UK. Combining learning time and holiday time in an exotic location with an expert tutor, the programmes allow participants to experience a place through travel writers' eyes whilst being guided by a leading professional. Breaks range from three to seven days of intensive exploration – of the destination and of your own creative potential. Choose from the colourful souks of Marrakech, the Berber villages of the Atlas Mountains, the vibrant streets of Istanbul, and the flamboyant Moorish cities of Andalusia. Creative learning is provided by two expert tutors on each trip. They lead live practice sessions in the location's top sites, supported by classroom seminars of theory and comment on your work in a group of kindred spirits sharing their interests and plans. Writing and photography courses are offered, allowing participants to do both courses should they wish to develop the full portfolio of creative skills. www.travellerstales.org

Women On Tour

This friendly all-female networking community run regular creative writing breaks to Istanbul and Barcelona and have tentative future plans to expand into South America. Inspirational workshops provide the support and confidence boost required by many women to take that leap of faith during a mix of short breaks and longer stays that involve high-calibre authors. www.womenontour.co.uk

FURTHER READING

A Sense of Place: Great Travel Writers Talk About Their Craft, Lives and Interests, Michael Shapiro (Travellers Tales).

A Writer's World: Travels (1950–2000), Jan Morris (Faber & Faber).

Best of Lonely Planet Travel Writing, Tony Wheeler (Lonely Planet).

British Travel Writers in Europe (1750–1800), Katherine Turner (Ashgate).

British Travel Writing from China (1798–1901), Elizabeth Chang (Pickering & Chatto Ltd).

Do Travel Writers Go to Hell? Thomas Kohnstamm (Potters Style).

How to Write and Sell Travel Articles, Cathy Smith (Rosiepress).

Imperial Eyes: Travel Writing and Transculturation, Mary Louise Pratt (Routledge).

Lonely Planet Guide to Travel Writing, David Else, Don George, and Charlotte Hindle (Lonely Planet).

The Best Travel Writing: True Stories from Around the World, James O'Reilly, Larry Habegger, and Sean O'Reilly (Travelers' Tales Inc.).

The Best Women's Travel Writing 2009, Lucy McCauley (Travellers' Tales Inc.).

The Cambridge Companion to Travel Writing, Peter Hulme and Tim Youngs (Cambridge University Press).

The Writers' Handbook Guide to Travel Writing, Barry Turner (Macmillan).

Tourists with Typewriters: Critical Reflections of Contemporary Travel Writing, Patric Holland (University of Michigan Press).

Travel Writing 1700–1830: An Anthology, Elizabeth Bohls and Ian Duncan (OUP Oxford).

Travel Writing and Empire: Post-Colonial Theory in Transit, Steve
   Clark (Zed Books Ltd).
Travel Writing: Major Writers Travel the Road, Linda Marsh and
   Michael Marland (Longman).
Travel Writing: See the World Sell the Story, L. Peat O'Neil
   (Writer's Digest Books).
Travel Writing: The New Critical Idiom, Carl Thompson (Routledge
   Publishing).
Travel Writing: The Self and The Word, Casey Blanton (Twayne
   Publishers Inc.).
*When You Smile You're Lying: Confessions of a Rogue Travel
   Writer*, Chuck Thompson (Holt).
Women Travel Writers and the Language of Aesthetics (1716–1818),
   Elizabeth Bohls (Cambridge University Press).

NETWORKING EVENTS

Adventure Travel Live

This full-on adventure travel extravaganza attracts exhibitors
from every aspect of independent travel, from tour operators
and guidebook publishers to tourist boards. Held each autumn,
Adventure Travel Live includes world food, music and arts and
has a good programme of networking events, talks and
presentations. Check the website for information.
www.adventureshow.co.uk

Business Travel & Meetings Show

Formally known as The Business Travel Show, this specialist
event was established 16 years ago and is held annually in
February at Earls Court in London. With hundreds of business
travel products, services and venues on show from the world's
leading suppliers as well as over 60 hours of quality education in
the expert-led conference, this is the number one dedicated event
for the business travel and meetings market. Members of the
travel media have an opportunity to see what's new, keep up to

date, meet brand new and traditional suppliers and network at a number of events. www.businesstravelshow.com

Cruise Travel Show

Run inconjunction with the *Daily Telegraph*, this annual cruise industry event in London is a must for anyone keen to write about travel on the high seas. Numerous exhibitors represent every aspect of the cruise sector and the show is a hive of activity in regards to networking, meetings, seminars and press events. www.telegraph.co.uk

Destinations

The UK's largest consumer travel and tourism show takes place in London and Birmingham, attracting thousands of exhibitors, members of the travel press and visitors alike. A staggering array of leading and independent travel companies provide inspiration, expert advice and exclusive offers at each Destinations show – together with press events and networking soirées. www.destinationsshow.com

Frankfurt Book Fair

The networking possibilities at the Frankfurt Book Fair make exciting reading in this international book event. Held annually, the fair hosts more than 7,300 exhibitors from over 100 countries and is the most important marketplace worldwide for books, media, rights and licences. Check the website for registration information. www.frankfurt-book-fair.com

London Book Fair (LBF)

This annual event is the global marketplace for rights negotiation and the sale and distribution of content across print, audio, TV, film and digital channels. Taking place every spring, the LBF provides authors with a unique opportunity to network in the vibrant atmosphere of this busy event and explore innovations shaping the publishing world. The LBF brings you direct access to customers, content and emerging markets and also hosts a number of seminars and networking

events. Check the website for registration information.
www.londonbookfair.co.uk

Luxury Travel Fair

This specialist high-end travel exhibition attracts a wide range
of specialists from that niche, from tour operators and tourist
boards to writers, journalists and authors.
www.luxurytravelfair.com

Travel Technology Show

Writers interested in travel technology will find a host of
experts at this specialist trade show as it attracts many of the
major players in the global technology sector for the travel
industry. Held each year in February, the Travel Technology
Show is a forum for education with over 70 exhibitors, a
focused seminar programme discussing the hottest topics
affecting the travel technology industry, free presentations such
as expert panel discussions and a Cimtig session on making
social networks work – as well as press events.
www.traveltechnologyshow.com

Women in Travel (WiT)

Founded by public relations firm Saltmarsh PR in 2007, Women
in Travel (WiT) is a networking collective of female
professionals from the travel sector. WiT events take place on a
quarterly basis and attract representatives of domestic and
international tourist boards, tour operators, airlines, other travel
organisations and the media. Industry support is strong, with
both international and domestic organisations having sponsored
and donated prizes for WiT evenings. www.saltmarshpr.co.uk/
women_in_travel.cfm

World Travel Market

This week-long trade event takes place immediately after the
British Guild of Travel Writers awards dinner in early
November. Almost every tour operator and tourist will run
some press event during WTM week – either at the venue or

after-hours in a restaurant, hotel or function suite elsewhere in London. Monday is Press Day. See the website for full details and registration process. www.wtmlondon.com

OTHER RESOURCES

British Guild of Travel Writers' Yearbook

Every year in February, the British Guild of Travel Writers (BGTW) publishes its 'bible' – a professionally produced who's who of the travel-writing scene and an indispensible guide for anyone involved in travel communications. Each member of the BGTW is profiled with details of their specialities and credentials, while every single tourist board, PR and travel trade contact is listed in detail in a directory of over 2,700 specialist PR companies, publications, broadcast media, tourist offices, tour and transport operators and other useful companies and organisations operating in the UK travel and tourism industry – making the Guild *Yearbook* a must for every travel writer, editor, photographer, broadcaster and author.

To order online, visit: http://www.bgtw.org/yearbook/index.php

Guidebookwriters.com

A sister organisation to Writers and Photographers Unlimited (WPU), this dedicated resource was established in 2004 to help authors of travel guidebooks market their skills and experience. At present it has over 50 of the world's best travel writers, offering online travel consultations, feature travel articles, and editorial resources for websites and publications. An annual fee applies. www.guidebookwriters.com

NUJ *Freelance Directory*

One of the most reliable and probably the biggest listing of professional English-language media freelances (as well as those who work in other areas) the *Freelance Directory* includes writers, editors, sub-editors, designers, illustrators, photographers, broadcasters, scriptwriters, web designers, translators, trainers and researchers working in over 20 countries. The *Directory* has been published by the National Union of Journalists since 1974 with listings free to members. www.freelancedirectory.org

Responsesource.com

This invaluable resource to writers and journalists allows them to post requests to thousands of PR specialists in the UK at express speed. Response Source is accessed using a simple form on the site. The recipients get the enquiries by email – quickly and efficiently. The requests are sent immediately and are structured carefully to allow PRs to decide rapidly whether a request is relevant and how they will respond. Journalists using Response Source love the rapid way they can send out a request for information out. It puts them back in control of the massive PR machine, which for too long seemed to simply 'push' information randomly to the press instead of responding individually to journalists' needs. Response Source is not designed to replace the journalist's contacts book or to compensate for poor research. Instead, it helps journalists gather quantities of information in a short time that would otherwise be impossible, allowing them to spend more time interviewing, investigating and writing.

Writers and Photographers Unlimited (WPU)

This online marketing service for English-language professional writers and photographers worldwide promotes the work, skills and experiences of its members to PR companies, tourist boards, editors, publishers and consultants. An annual fee applies. www.wpu.org.uk

Appendix 3

Travel Writing Samples

Wind Surf, by Gary Buchanan
Published in *World of Cruising*, 2009

Fulfilling a long-held ambition, I hailed a taxi and asked him to take me to Maho Beach. Whilst no one could dispute the Dutch side is less attractive than the French, it is here that the island's main international airport lies – with the end of the runway just a few feet from the wonderful sandy beach. A pizza lunch amongst a gaggle of avid plane-spotters at the Sunset Bar preceded the European flight arrivals. Standing underneath a colossal Air France Airbus as it swept on to the runway was a most surreal experience. The landing gear hanging down from the fuselage was like a pterodactyl's claws about to clutch the bystanders and the noise was deafening.

With a late sailing I invited a delightful English girl to dinner in the achingly beautiful resort of Grand Case. At a beachside table in the impossibly romantic L'Escapade restaurant we dined on foie gras and sea bass. It was during *digestifs* that she admitted to being passionate about Star Clippers. A nautical banter ensued and we agreed that the differing designations of the two types of ships sum the dichotomy up nicely: whilst Wind Star vessels are referred to as MSY (Motor Sailing Yacht), the square-rigged Star Clippers are denoted SPV (Sailing Passenger Vessel). In fact by the end of our cruise one or more of the sails had been deployed for a total of just 43 hours.

The French flavour continued the following day. Of all the Caribbean islands, none is invested with quite the mystique of tiny St Barthélemy, eight square miles of steep green hills, sugary beaches, and legendary Gallic charm. A Dorian Gray version of France four thousand miles west of the Champs Elyseés, this volcanic outcrop stays youthful while the real thing ages. The colourful market in the bijou capital Gustavia is a vignette of France where imported wines, cheeses and breads are displayed. Elsewhere Prada beachwear and Cartier jewellery are on display in the doll-size boutiques that line the streets of this palm-fringed outpost of Empire. It was here my new companion reciprocated lunch at Le Sélect – the original yachters' hangout commemorated in Jimmy Buffet's 'Cheeseburger in Paradise'.

Another side of the French Caribbean revealed itself the following day in Basse-Terre, capital of Guadeloupe. Far from chic, this bustling city's ramshackle streets were choked by cars and the spice market staffed by locals overflowing in insouciance. The genial nature of the Windward Islands was re-established when a local school choir sang as we sailed the short distance to Terre-de-Haut in the Iles des Saintes. As the sails started to billow in the winds and we nudged further out to sea, their joyous singing gave way to our own sailaway anthem: Vangelis' rousing theme tune '1492 – The Conquest of Paradise'; played during every departure on the ship's loudspeakers.

As we sailed that evening we gazed at the calm, but sensuously undulating sea. The next day would be our final port and a beach barbecue was scheduled on Pigeon Island off the north-western tip of St Lucia. A marvellous steel band whose players beat the pans and spun like whirling dervishes accompanied a sun-kissed day of watersports and lotus-eating. As the sun slowly began taking its leave we navigated along the coast of this island with its sugar-loaf mountains until we reached the impossibly photogenic Pitons. It was a perfect conclusion to a cruise through a sequestered pattern of islands that left an indelible mosaic of dreams.

Gary Buchanan has been a travel writer for the past 22 years and for most of that time has been a specialist cruise writer. He regularly contributes to The Times, The Telegraph, World of Cruising, Cruise International, *and* Cruise Traveller. *He is the author of four maritime books and used to lecture on board the QE2 about the history of the cruise industry. He has sailed with almost every cruise line across the Seven Seas but especially enjoys expedition-style cruising to remote areas.*

Want to Save the Planet? Pick up Your Towels,
by Helen Truszkowski
Published by The Independent Online, 2005

Like island destinations everywhere, those in the Caribbean are a
fragile paradise. The pressure created by droves of holidaymakers
and their increasing demands is leaving a depressing litany of
damage. According to the World Resources Institute, two-thirds
of the Caribbean's beaches are already eroded; wildlife is being
displaced by huge hotel complexes, water sports cause coastal,
coral-reef and marine pollution, while more and more wetlands
are being destroyed to develop golf courses.

Sure, if you're anything like me, you go on holiday to have a good
time, not to save the world. But, be honest, wouldn't you like to
know your family break could be about giving, not just taking?

Well, take heart. Ecotourism is going mainstream, and the
Caribbean is feeling the effect. Take Tobago's Blue Haven Hotel
(001 868 660 7400; www.bluehavenhotel.com), an antidote to so
many of the fenced-off and homogenised resorts in the region. It
is renowned for several things: incredible food, a spectacular, film-
star setting and, above all, its commitment to the happy marriage
of ecology and tourism.

It wasn't always so. A heyday haunt for the likes of Rita Hayworth
and Robert Mitchum, the hotel lay abandoned for more than 25
years. Planning a complete renovation, its new owners were
committed to both preserving the original architecture and
installing modern environmentally-friendly measures.

The result is stunning thirties colonial chic underpinned by a nature-conscious strategy. The hotel uses solar heating, biodegradable detergents, energy-saving gadgets, rainwater irrigation, plus local, organically grown produce and toiletries. It has also banned polluting motor water sports. Only local staff are employed there, and the scale of the hotel is kept small enough to safeguard the highest quality service and lowest impact tourism.

Glitter Bay in Barbados (001 246 422 5555; www.fairmont.com/glitterbay) is equally grand, with impeccably furnished rooms, a crisply uniformed staff and immaculate lawns. Children are welcome, with club activities scheduled throughout the day and a pool of nannies on tap. On a recent family visit, my son helped monitor hawksbill turtle nest-sites, went on a scavenger hunt for throwaway plastics that threaten the marine life and spent time at one of the local schools the resort has adopted. Meanwhile, Glitter Bay's dedicated Green Team got to grips with waste management, donating used hotel crockery to local hospitals, composting garden waste and recycling bed covers into pillow shams. The aim is to saturate Caribbean holiday spots with a renewed beauty that's more than skin deep.

Freelance travel writer, author and photograher Helen Truszkowski writes for a wide range of newspapers and magazines including The Independent on Sunday, The Times, The Daily Express, The Sunday Express *and* Geographical. *She has also appeared on Radio 5 Live, the BBC and The Discovery Channel.*
Visit: www.helentruszkowski.com.

Greek Chic, by Liz Jarvis
Published by *Shape* magazine, 2008

There can be few places better for getting your head together than
the Acropolis. Standing high above Athens, surrounded by the
ancient sun-bleached marble ruins of the Parthenon, a gentle
breeze on your skin as you gaze at the glittering sea on the
horizon puts everything into perspective. No wonder so many
Ancient Greeks once peddled their philosophies up here.

Athens used to be one of those cities you visited on a pre-booked
whistle-stop coach tour, just killing time while waiting for your
plane home after a fortnight of island-hopping. Not any more.
It's cleaner (really), it's safe, it's got culture and history oozing
out of every brick, and brilliant nightlife.

It's never going to be chocolate-box pretty, but olive and (non-
edible) orange trees line the wide pavements, there are hundreds
of stylish new shops and restaurants, and when the sun sets on the
Acropolis, with the sky all purple-gold, it's breathtaking. The
whole city buzzes with an infectious energy that makes you
naturally higher than any ouzo.

All the main sights are in close proximity. A good starting point is
Syntagma Square, where, guarding the Tomb of the Unknown
Soldier outside the Parliament Building, are the mini-skirted
Evzones. It's worth waiting to see them perform their patrol.
From here you can easily walk to Hadrian's Arch.

The metro is the best way to get around the city – unless you're feeling energetic and the sun isn't too hot when you visit (there's a lot of uphill walking). One of the reasons everything takes so long to build in Athens is that every time they start digging, they uncover more ruins, and many of them are on display in the metro. But try to hail a taxi at least once – it's an entertaining, if bumpy ride.

London-based journalist and editor Liz Jarvis has been writing about travel for over ten years, contributing features to a range of magazines, websites and newspapers including Shape, Real, love it!, Closer, Top Santé, Tesco, The Sun *and the* Irish Daily Mirror. *She can be contacted via lizjarvis1@yahoo.co.uk.*

Bush Baby, by Mike Unwin
Published in *Africa Geographic Magazine*, June 2008

'Don't *want* to look!' comes the tearful protest from the booster seat.

'But darling, it's a giraffe. Your favourite', I plead from the front, now flagging.

'Hate giraffes! Giraffes are boring!'

This isn't supposed to happen. Back home in the UK, during the long months planning our big family trip to Africa, I had cherished the prospect of our first game drive in the Kruger Park. This was to be the moment that raised the curtain on African wildlife for my four-year-old daughter. It would, I had no doubt, ignite in her the same lifelong obsession that had long ago claimed her father.

And I know that she loves African animals. How can she not? Like all western children of her age, she has grown up on cuddly lions, happy hippos and cheeky meerkats. Even her alphabet ends in 'zebra'. Now, at last, I'm showing her the real thing. Forget all those toys and DVDs; forget Lion Kings and Gruffalos: this is a living, breathing, five-metre-tall giraffe. You can see its glistening saliva strung among the acacia thorns.

So why the tears? Doesn't she know how lucky she is?

The trip had started well enough, with wildlife illuminating our journey around the South African coast. On Boulders Beach we had waddled with the penguins, at De Hoop we had waved back at the tail flukes of a southern right, and at Storms River we had teased the tentacles of an octopus from its rock pool lair. So far, so good. Now, three weeks later, we were ready for the main event: the *Real Africa*.

And this, I now realise, was the problem. Our itinerary was all of *my* making: an adult's idea of the perfect Africa trip. To my mind, the giraffe was more than just an animal: it embodied the romantic, untamed allure of a whole continent. But my daughter, unencumbered by such baggage, was simply tired of being stuck in the car. The protracted I-spy game had long since run its course and now nothing, not even a Little Mermaid at the next waterhole, could get her excited. When could she get out and run around? When could she have an icecream?

Happily the Kruger was not a disaster. We soon picked up some survival basics: you can't expect your child's agenda to coincide with your own, for a start; and there is only so long you can sustain the interest of a four-year-old imprisoned in a vehicle, no matter what's on view from the window.

Mike Unwin divides his time between editing natural history books, writing, photography, and illustration. He won the BBC Wildlife/ Bradt Travel Guides Travel-Writing Competition. Living in Zimbabwe and Swaziland allowed him to explore southern Africa. Mike is also the editor of Travel Zambia *magazine.*
Visit: www.bgtw.org/mike-unwin.html.

Into Yukon's Kluane National Park, by Polly Evans
Published by greatoutdoors.com, 2009

The three of us stood stripped to our underwear and contemplated the rushing glacial stream. The water came to hip height – if we wanted to stay dry we'd have to undress still further – but wordlessly we agreed to cling to this one last vestige of propriety. And then, backpack waist straps unclipped in case of calamity and using each other's bodies for support, we inched our way through the numbing torrents.

This was the last morning of our nine-day hike along the Donjek Route, a spectacular 80-mile loop past the Donjek Glacier in Kluane National Park in Canada's Yukon Territory. Together with the adjoining parks of Tatshenshini – Alsek in British Columbia and Wrangell – St. Elias and Glacier Bay in Alaska, Kluane (pronounced Kloo-AH-nee) comprises 38,000 square miles of unbroken wilderness: that's almost the size of the state of Kentucky. For the last nine days we hadn't seen another human soul. But while the interior of this vast backcountry is seldom imprinted by the heavy boots of bipeds, it's a popular stamping ground for grizzly and black bears, wolves, lynx, mountain goats, and moose. The park is home to the largest concentration of Dall's sheep in the world, as well as more than 150 bird species including trumpeter swans, peregrine falcons and gyrfalcons, and bald and golden eagles.

The Donjek Route, Parks Canada emphasizes, is not a trail. 'Wilderness travel experience is essential, including excellent route finding skills, map and compass skills, and creek/river crossing skills', the rangers insist in their literature. I had none of these estimable qualities. However, the other two in my party – my guide Stefan, from Whitehorse-based adventure company Nature Tours of Yukon, and his girlfriend Cynthia – were made of stern muscles and sterling map-interpreting stuff, and seven years in British boarding schools had bestowed on me a stiff upper lip and an unwillingness to complain.

Work by Polly Evans has appeared in magazines and newspapers including the Sunday Times, The Times, The Independent on Sunday, Wanderlust, Condé Nast Traveller, BBC Wildlife Magazine, High Life *and* Food & Wine. *In 2006, she won the Independent on Sunday/Bradt Travel Guides travel-writing competition. Polly has also written five books about her travels across New Zealand, Spain, China, Argentina and Canada's Yukon Territory. Visit. www.pollyevans.com*

Russian Saga, by Robin Mead
Published by the *Jewish Chronicle*, Feb 2009

The shoulders of the man who bears responsibility for the deaths of millions of people, and the enslavement of millions more, are reassuringly narrow. He sits at his desk with his hands gripping the arms of his chair, as if trying to explain himself. Even the fact that he is seated cannot hide the fact that, for a man who had such a big impact on the modern world, Josef Stalin was surprisingly small.

Stalin – or at least a lifelike waxwork model of the man – lives on in the Russian Black Sea resort of Sochi, where his 'dacha', or summer residence, is the solitary tourist attraction.

Like Sochi itself, Stalin's dacha is remarkably uncrowded. Half-hidden on a wooded hillside above the town, and painted green as a form of camouflage, the house is a large square constructed round a central courtyard garden. Stalin far preferred the peace and safety of this house to the Kremlin, and the dacha has been left much as it was in his day.

Moreover the Russians, so paranoid in many other ways, are remarkably relaxed about tourists visiting the dacha. You can touch the personal items on his desk, sit on his uncomfortable horsehair sofa (with its armoured back, to guard against assassins), play on his billiards table or even use his personal toilet – no-one will even murmur a protest.

Sadly, visiting the dacha is about all you can do in Sochi. If you haven't got a personal visa (and fewer than one per cent of the passengers on my Saga cruise to the Black Sea had), then the Russians will not let you off the ship except on an organised and accompanied coach excursion. Want to visit a street market, meet the locals, soak up the atmosphere? Not a chance.

But Sochi is an exception. Russia's Black Sea neighbours – especially Romania and Ukraine – are very keen to welcome cruise passengers to their shores. So much so, in fact, that it is surprising how few ex-UK cruises go there every year.

Despite the Saga image, plenty of my fellow passengers on 'Saga Rose' were ready to shake a leg with local dancers as we arrived in Constanza, and the ship itself is a thoroughbred. Saga promote their cruises as having three big advantages over rivals: 'real' ships, single-sitting meals, and no children on board. On a voyage of exploration like this, I'll drink to all three!

London-based Robin Mead is a former British Guild of Travel Writers' chairman. He has written for magazines and newspapers all over the world; Robin now focuses on river and deep sea cruising. www.robinmead.com and is the author of 24 travel guide books.

North to Alaska, by Roger Norum
Published by The Guardian Online, 2008

As we slink the RV into the campground, Dad, several weeks from retirement but still solid, is already on the phone. 'No, nothing really... Just that we've arrived at the middle of nowhere, and that tomorrow we're headed somewhere, but nowhere in particular.' Our days driving the Alcan Highway seem to exist for the sole purpose of cracking Abbott and Costello punch lines. The corny phone calls to Mum are starting to grate on me.

In a car-smitten continent of service-stop strip malls and turnpike Wal-Marts, the Alaska-Canadian Highway – the Alcan – is a curiosity: a true wilderness thoroughfare. From Dawson Creek, British Columbia, to Fairbanks, Alaska, the asphalt and gravel road hurtles and plunges through 1,500 miles of alpine buttes, black spruce forests and carpeted plains of tussock and tundra. Chuckholes, ripples and washboard humps created by the perennial freezing and thawing of the surrounding land make for roller-coaster driving.

Fifty years ago, just after the US Senate voted to make Alaska the 49th state, Dad drove the Alcan with Grandpa in an orange Volkswagen camper. The stories from that trip – fishing for sockeye salmon, swimming in the Yukon, roasting caribou under the stars – had long drawn me to this part of the world. I've returned with Dad to retrace their journey, upping the ante with a vehicle that makes the VW look like a Vespa. The innards of our rented mega-RV include a shower, toilet, microwave, toaster, full-

size beds and two kitchen sinks. If you've ever helmed an oil
tanker, manning a vehicle this size won't feel too foreign.

At the wheel, Dad prefers slow-paced driving on cruise control;
my motorus operandi is pedal to the metal. And we each take
turns at backseat driving. 'Slow and steady wins the race', he'll
caution me as I hightail it through the Canadian hinterland. 'He
who hesitates is lost', I'll snark back at him as river salmon
outpace us.

When not trading platitudes, we share in the wonder of the
North, OHH-ing and WOW-ing at the otherworldly landscapes, as
families of Dall sheep and moose wander moon-like glacial hills
and S-shaped rivers. It's an experience amplified by the extended
summer hours of near-Arctic daylight, an unsettling phenomenon
that deceives the senses: driving without headlamps at 10pm; a
glowing red sunset at midnight; waking up to a 'dawn' chorus of
birdsong at 3am.

*New Yorker Roger Norum has spent extended periods
in Scandinavia, India, Hong Kong, Argentina, Mongolia, Tajikistan
and the UK. Together with broadcast work for CBS Radio News, he
writes for various newspapers and magazines, including* The Los
Angeles Times, The Guardian, The Independent *and* The Oxford
Student. *Roger is fluent in French, Norwegian, Russian and
Spanish, proficient in Arabic, Italian, Mandarin Chinese and
Turkish and has conversational knowledge of a few others. Since
moving to the UK in 2004, he has contributed as a writer and
photographer to ten separate Rough Guide titles, three of which he
has either co-authored or authored.*

From Hull, Hell and Halifax may the good Lord deliver us!, by Rosemary Bailey

Returning to Yorkshire last week, the names began to reverberate from distant memory; Hebden Bridge, Wensleydale, Ilkley Moor, Whitby. I could hear my father's long Northern vowels again, and recall his ringing sermons. 'From Hell, Hull and Halifax' was a great joke between Walter and his non-conformist buddies. But only now have I discovered that it was a 17th century thieves' litany – Hull because there was a notorious gaol there, and Halifax because of its famous gibbet, a precursor of the guillotine though with the curious distinction of being operated with a rope which all could grasp, a fair administration of rough justice. Very Yorkshire, perhaps.

I anticipated the trip to Yorkshire with some curiosity, never having visited the county of my birth as a tourist. They used to call it 'God's own county', and remain as proud of it as ever. It was like visiting a different country, more foreign now to me than France. Industrial has become post-industrial with some noted successes, the 1853 gallery at Saltaire, a huge mill now home to David Hockney's paintings, the Deep aquarium in Hull, the textile mills turned into luxurious eco-spas.

But it was in the enduring landscape that I felt once again at home; the elemental beauty of the moors, rushing waters, undulating valleys stitched with rugged stone walls and scattered with hardy black-faced Wensleydale sheep. Most of all the wild skies moving with clouds above. I grew up with plenty of sky.

Author, writer and blogger Rosemary Bailey is a seasoned traveller and a British Guild of Travel Writers award winner. This is an excerpt from her travel blog. Visit: www.rosemarybailey.com.

Skiing in Luxury, by Victoria Trott
Published in Raymond Blanc's *Seasons* magazine, Winter, 2008

The chairlift glides towards a sugar-dusted peak as you snuggle into your cashmere snood to keep out the cold, winter air. Below, a carpet of white powder covers the valley floor; wood and stone chalets huddle together around the village centre. Above, an intense, bright sun hangs in a vibrant, blue sky; the only sound to be heard is the wind whistling past your ears.

Soon, after bouncing along for the last few metres, it's time to jump off; the excitement rises as you anticipate your first run of the year. Yes, it's the ski season again and, while such zen experiences let you leave your cares behind, with it comes the eternal problem of deciding where to go – so here's a look at three of the world's best and most stylish resorts.

Mention the name Klosters and the first thing that springs to mind is Royalty: the Prince of Wales and his inner circle have been holidaying in this charming Swiss village for years, along with socialite Tara Palmer-Tomkinson, who has a chalet here.

At the foot of the busy Parsenn ski area, Klosters is often called the smaller, more attractive sister of Davos – Europe's highest town and host of the annual World Economic Forum. In total, the Davos-Klosters resort extends over 190 miles and covers six separate areas, which are easily accessible by bus, train and lifts.

But it's not just a pretty face: the resort is a mecca for intermediate and advanced skiers as more than 70 per cent of its slopes are red and black, with some excellent long runs back to the village. Experienced snowboarders should head to Jakobshorn for some challenging off-piste and two half-pipes while for novices, there are two highly regarded ski and board schools in Bolgen, at the foot of the mountain. Those who like their action to be a little more fluid should trek over to Pischa, as last season it became a piste-free freeride zone.

Wales-based freelance travel writer and photographer Victoria Trott has travelled extensively in France, Spain and Greece. Her adventures have taken her from the dizzy heights of working as PA to an American billionaire at a luxury villa on the French Riviera, to the grim depths of being a general dogsbody at a bug-infested Greek yoga retreat. She writes for the Daily Mail, Living France *and* Spain Magazine *and is co-author of Frommer's* Provence & the Cote d'Azur with Your Family. *Visit: www.victoriatrott.com.*

On The Truffle Trail, by Lisa Gerard-Sharp
Published in *Italia!* Magazine, 2009

Aphrodisiac or not, the Alba white truffle oozes sex appeal. My nose recoils from the truffle aromas. It's akin to being plunged into a farmyard reeking of manure, mouldy compost, mushrooms, methane, musk, muddy clods of earth. The second whiff is pure pheromones, essence of sex – all emanating from this ugly, wizened knob.

I love it, as do the panting truffle dogs sharing the moment with me. White truffles do this to people, twist your language into soft porn. 'Truffles taste and smell of people and sweat', says celebrity chef Giorgio Locatelli, 'Everything that life tastes and smells of is in there.'

Just another Monday morning at truffle school in Montechiaro d'Asti, in the misty oak groves of southern Piedmont. Giuseppe, as wizened as the white truffle he's holding aloft, is getting into his stride with the life-sex-and-death theme that truffle-hunters adore. 'We have a saying that these "white diamonds" carry the powers to make women more tender and men more virile. But the best death for this truffle is on my plate.' He conjures up images of steaming *tajerin* pasta flecked with potent truffle shavings. Unfortunately, it's wishful thinking. Eating a white Alba truffle is like putting a gold ring on your risotto. More costly than gold or diamonds, Alba's white truffles are rarely eaten by the *trufulau,* the truffle-hunters who scour the wintry fields with their faithful dogs.

Umbria boasts black truffles, but they pale into insignificance beside the superior white truffle from around Piedmont. *Tuber Magnatum Pico* is the grand name for the gnarled lump that draws some of the world's greatest chefs to Alba every autumn. As pungent as it is pricey, the white truffle is a paradox. It is a princely treat that has been harvested by peasants since Roman times. 'What's so special about white truffles?' asks a late-comer to the hunt. 'If you have to ask, you haven't sniffed one, you haven't lived' is Giuseppe's curt reply.

We're still marooned in the mists of our daytime truffle hunt. As the mists lift, the ghostly white cattle float past our field of vision with a lumbering grace. This is a simulated truffle hunt, so, rather like simulated sex, isn't quite the same thing. Yet it invariably ends in a small death. The ghostly white cattle and the ghostly white truffle – both beauties end up on the plate, one as *carpaccio antipasti* and the other grated over pasta.

As an independent-minded travel writer, foreign correspondent, feature-writer, lifestyle journalist, author and editor, Lisa Gerard-Sharp contributes to magazines, national newspapers, guidebooks, TV and travel websites worldwide. Although she is British, her cosmopolitan background includes an Italian partner, an Australian mother, American sisters and an Armenian sister-in-law – all useful travel writing resources when she runs short of ideas.
Visit: www.bgtw.org/lisa-gerard-sharp.html.

Index